ASIANHIGHTEA
FAVOURITES

ASIAN HIGH TEA FAVOURITES

BETTY SAW

TIMES EDITIONS

For this book, the publisher wishes to thank **Robinsons & Co** and **Java Enterprises Pte Ltd** for the loan and use of their tableware.

Managing Editor : Jamilah Mohd Hassan
Editor : Selina Kuo
Art Direction/Designer : Cynthia Ng
Photographers : Joshua Tan & Cedric Lim
Recipe Tester : Cheong Mee Siew
Production Co-ordinator : Nor Sidah Haron

First published 1979
Reprinted 1981, 1982, 1983, 1986, 1993, 1995
This new edition 2004

Published by Times Editions – Marshall Cavendish
An imprint of Marshall Cavendish International (Asia) Private Limited
A member of the Times Publishing Limited

Times Centre, 1 New Industrial Road, Singapore 536196
Tel: (65) 6213 9288 Fax: (65) 6285 4871
E-mail: te@sg.marshallcavendish.com
Online Bookstore: http://www.timesone.com.sg/te

Malaysian Office:
Federal Publications Sdn Bhd (General & Reference Publishing) (3024-D)
Times Subang, Lot 46, Persiaran Teknologi Subang
Subang Hi-Tech Industrial Park
Batu Tiga, 40000 Shah Alam
Selangor Darul Ehsan, Malaysia
Tel: (603) 5635 2191 Fax: (603) 5635 2706
E-mail: cchong@tpg.com.my

National Library Board (Singapore) Cataloguing in Publication Data

Saw, Betty
Asian high tea favourites / Betty Saw. – New ed. – Singapore : Times Editions, 2004.
p. cm.
First published: Times Books International, c1979.
ISBN 981-232-606-5

1. Afternoon teas. 2. Confectionery. 3. Cake. 4. Cookery, Southeast Asian. I. Title.

TX736
641.53 – dc21 SLS2004012510

Printed in Singapore by Times Printers Pte Ltd

To

Doreen,

Shareen

and Gary

CONTENTS

FOREWORD

The very word "tea" carries with it memories of mouth-watering, scrumptious cakes, delicious savouries, golden crunchy loaves and buns, a blissful spread of cookies, light delicate pastries and luscious sweets.

I have enjoyed time and time again recipes which are now complied in this book. They have gathered our families and friends to share many good times and celebrated occasions. They have been thoroughly enjoyed by all and I feel certain they will be enjoyed with equal enthusiasm and relish if you try them yourself. At the same time, you'll be passing on to your family, friends and guests a store of memories of the taste of simple, good home baking and cooking in the relaxed atmosphere of your own home.

This book contains not only delectable familiar recipes, but also many exciting and imaginative creations and decorations.

I have thoroughly enjoyed working through this book and I hope you'll make the most of it. I also hope that the book will prove to be an incentive and inspiring source in your own kitchen and that you'll find fun and pleasure in all your attempts.

Acknowledgements

I am indeed indebted and grateful to my family and friends for their full support, unfailing encouragement and interest. They have graciously and generously contributed their help in numerous ways to make this book possible.

Cooking Hints

Always preheat the oven to the specified temperature before baking.

Always use castor (superfine) sugar when a recipe calls for it because undissolved sugar granules following inadequate creaming lead to white specks on the cake's surface.

Always use large eggs for making cakes and at room temperature because they produce a greater volume after beating than cold eggs of the same size.

- Large eggs 70–75 g
- Medium eggs 60–65 g
- Small eggs 55 g

When whisking eggs and sugar, beat at a high speed until the mixture is thick and white.

Always cleanly separate egg yolks and whites. Drops of egg yolk in egg whites can easily be removed with half an egg shell.

When adding eggs to a creamed mixture, be careful not to do it too quickly as curdling will result. Should curdling occur, however, add a little flour.

When folding in the flour in sponge cakes, do it quickly as air bubbles in the mixture will otherwise break. Air that has been beaten into the mixture and trapped in the form of bubbles is what gives sponge cakes the light and even texture.

Always thoroughly mix batter scraped from the sides of the bowl with the rest of the bowl's contents as uneven mixing will lead to differently coloured streaks on the cake's surface.

Cooking Hints

When making self-raising flour at home, add 2 tsp baking powder to every 120 g plain (all-purpose) flour.

When baking, avoid opening the oven door during the first 20 minutes as sudden rushes of cooler air can cause a cake to sink. Overheating an oven can also cause a cake to sink because the mixture has been forced to rise too quickly.

When leaving a sponge cake out to cool, make sure that it is not placed in a spot that experiences rushes of cooler air as the cake will shrink and wrinkle as a result. Undercooked sponge cakes also shrink and wrinkle.

Always check that a cake is thoroughly cooked before removing it from the oven. A good test is to insert a skewer into the centre of the cake, and if the skewer comes out clean, then the cake is ready to be taken out of the oven.

When serving sponge cakes, remember that they taste best on the day that they have been baked. Butter cakes keep well for a few days in airtight containers, while gingerbread and fruit cakes improve in flavour over time.

Always store cakes and biscuits in separate containers. When stored together, the biscuits will become soft.

Always check that the yeast being used is fresh. Fresh yeast is beige-white in colour and should rise and turn frothy within 10–15 minutes of being lowered into lukewarm milk or water. Otherwise, yeast is stale. Recipes in this book use fresh or reconstituted milk.

Always make sure that water in the steamer is boiling before steaming.

There is
no love sincerer
than the love of food.

George Bernard Shaw
Man and Superman

cakes

Preparation time: 45 minutes; Baking time: 40 minutes
Oven setting: 175°C, 350°F, Gas Regulo 6

PINEAPPLE UPSIDE-DOWN CAKE

INGREDIENTS

Pineapple rings	9
Red cherries	5, halved
Butter	250 g, cold and diced
Castor (superfine) sugar	225 g
Eggs	4, large
Vanilla essence (extract)	1 tsp
Self-raising flour	240 g
Pineapple juice	1–2 Tbsp
Pineapple cream*	1 recipe

METHOD

- Line a 22-cm square cake tin with greased greaseproof paper. Arrange pineapple rings in three rows of three to cover base of tin. Place a cherry half in the centre of each ring.
- Cream butter and sugar until light and creamy. Add eggs one at a time. Add vanilla essence. Sift in half the flour and fold into mixture. Repeat with other half. Add pineapple juice to achieve soft, dropping consistency.
- Carefully spread batter over top of pineapple rings. Bake on centre shelf for 40–45 minutes or until skewer inserted into cake's centre comes out clean. Turn out and leave to cool on a wire rack.
- Decorate cake as desired with pineapple cream.

*Pineapple Cream

INGREDIENTS:

Butter	250 g, cold and cut into small pieces
Icing (confectioners') sugar	150 g, sifted
Vanilla essence (extract)	1 tsp
Evaporated milk	175 ml, cold
Pineapple juice	2 Tbsp, cold

METHOD:

- Beat butter pieces with sugar until light and creamy. Add vanilla essence. Beat in milk a little at a time. Beat in pineapple juice.

APPLE CAKE

INGREDIENTS

Brown sugar	2–3 Tbsp
Plain (all-purpose) flour (A)	2 Tbsp, sifted
Ground cinnamon	2 tsp
Apples	4, peeled, cored and evenly sliced
Eggs	4, large
Castor (superfine) sugar	225 g
Corn oil	250 ml
Vanilla essence (extract)	1 tsp
Salt	1 pinch
Water	150–180 ml, cold
Plain (all-purpose) flour (B)	300 g
Baking powder	2 tsp

METHOD

- Line a 22-cm square cake tin with greased greaseproof paper.
- Combine brown sugar, flour (A) and ground cinnamon in a bowl. Toss apple slices in bowl's contents. Set aside.
- Whisk eggs and sugar. Add corn oil, vanilla essence, salt and water. Sift in flour (B) and baking powder.
- Pour half the batter into prepared tin. Arrange apple slices on top. Spread remaining batter over apple slices to barely cover them. It does not matter if slices stick out.
- Bake for 45–60 minutes.

Preparation time: 20 minutes; Baking time: 75 minutes
Oven setting: 165°C, 325°F, Gas Regulo 5

ORANGE CHIFFON CAKE

INGREDIENTS

Plain (all-purpose) flour	240 g
Baking powder	1 Tbsp
Castor (superfine) sugar	300 g
Corn oil	125 ml
Eggs	7, separated into yolks and whites
Orange rind	grated from 2 oranges
Orange juice or water	125 ml
Salt	1/2 tsp
Cream of tartar	1/2 tsp

METHOD

- Line the base of a 27 x 9-cm tube pan with greased greaseproof paper.
- Sift flour and baking powder together. Set aside.
- Beat sugar in corn oil. Add egg yolks. Beat until smooth. Add orange rind and juice or water. Fold in sifted ingredients quickly, together with salt. Set aside.
- Whisk cream of tartar and egg whites until stiff but not dry. Gently and gradually pour egg-yolk mixture over beaten egg whites. Mix evenly.
- Pour batter into prepared pan. Bake on lowest shelf for 75 minutes or until cake is springy to the touch.

Preparation time: 30 minutes; Baking time: 75 minutes
Oven setting: 165°C, 325°F, Gas Regulo 5

SANTAN CHIFFON CAKE

INGREDIENTS

Plain (all-purpose) flour	240 g
Baking powder	1 Tbsp
Eggs	6, separated into yolks and whites
Sugar	280 g
Salt	1/4 tsp
Coconut milk	225 ml, squeezed from 1 grated coconut and sufficient water
Screwpine (*pandan*) juice	1 Tbsp, from pounding and squeezing screwpine leaves
Green food colouring	a few drops
Cream of tartar	1/2 tsp
Corn oil	2 tsp

METHOD

- Sift flour and baking powder together, twice. Set aside.
- Beat egg yolks, sugar and salt until white and creamy. Add coconut milk, screwpine juice and food colouring. Sift in sifted ingredients. Fold in quickly but lightly.
- Whisk cream of tartar and egg whites until soft peaks form. Pour egg-yolk mixture over whisked egg whites. Mix lightly and evenly. Stir in corn oil.
- Pour batter into a well-greased 25 x 9-cm tube pan. Bake for 75 minutes.
- When done, invert onto a wire rack straightaway. Remove tin after 5 minutes.

Preparation time: 15 minutes; Baking time: 50 minutes
Oven setting: 175°C, 350°F, Gas Regulo 6

PEAR CAKE

INGREDIENTS

Plain (all-purpose) flour	180 g
Baking powder	1 tsp
Pear	1, medium–large, peeled, cored and evenly sliced
Brown sugar (A)	60 g
Butter	180 g
Brown sugar (B)	150 g
Eggs	2
Brandy	2 Tbsp
Brown sugar (extra)	quantity as desired

METHOD

- Line a 20-cm round cake tin with greased greaseproof paper.
- Sift flour and baking powder together. Set aside.
- Toss pear slices in sugar (A). Set aside.
- Cream butter and sugar (B) until light and fluffy. Add eggs one at a time, beating well after each addition. Fold in sifted ingredients, together with brandy.
- Spread batter in prepared tin evenly. Arrange pear slices on batter's surface. Bake for 50 minutes.
- When done, sprinkle extra brown sugar over the top while still hot.

Preparation time: 15 minutes; Baking time: 50 minutes
Oven setting: 175°C, 350°F, Gas Regulo 6

NICE AND SPICY GINGERBREAD

INGREDIENTS

Eggs	2, large
Plain (all-purpose) flour	90 g
Self-raising flour	90 g
Bicarbonate (baking) of soda	1 tsp
Ground ginger	2 tsp
Ground cinnamon	1/2 tsp
Mixed spice	1/2 tsp
Salt	1 pinch
Sugar	225 g
Milk	225 ml
Corn oil	125 ml
Golden syrup	175 ml

METHOD

- Line a 20–22-cm square cake tin with two layers of greaseproof paper. Grease top layer and set aside.
- Using an electric mixer, whisk eggs for 3 minutes or until frothy.
- Sift powdered ingredients together into a mixing bowl. Add salt, sugar, milk, and whisked eggs. Mix well.
- Mix corn oil and golden syrup together. Stir syrup mixture into batter. Stir until well combined.
- Pour batter into prepared tin. Bake for 50 minutes or until cake is springy to the touch.

Preparation time: 15 minutes; Baking time: 25 minutes
Oven setting: 175°C, 350°F, Gas Regulo 6

MOCHA CAKE

INGREDIENTS

Cocoa (unsweetened)	2 Tbsp
Instant coffee	1 Tbsp
Bicarbonate of (baking) soda	1/2 tsp
Water	60 ml
Corn oil	125 ml
Castor (superfine) sugar	170 g
Vanilla essence (extract)	1 tsp
Eggs	3, large
Self-raising flour	240 g, sifted
Salt	1/2 tsp
Milk	2 Tbsp

METHOD

- Line a 20-cm square tin with greased greaseproof paper.
- Combine cocoa, instant coffee, bicarbonate of soda and water. Set aside.
- Beat corn oil, sugar, and vanilla essence. Add eggs one at a time. Beat in cocoa mixture. Sift in sifted flour. Add salt. Stir in milk.
- Pour batter into prepared tin and bake for 25 minutes. When done, transfer to a wire rack to cool.

Preparation time: 15 minutes; Baking time: 50 minutes
Oven setting: 175°C, 350°F, Gas Regulo 6

APPLE CHEESECAKE

INGREDIENTS

Brown sugar	75 g
Ground cinnamon	1/2 tsp
Red apples	3, medium, peeled, cored, and evenly sliced
Plain (all-purpose) flour	150 g
Baking powder	1 tsp
Sugar	115 g
Eggs	2
Corn oil	115 ml
Vanilla essence (extract)	1/2 tsp
Salt	1 pinch
Cheese topping*	1 recipe

METHOD

- Grease a 21-cm round springform cake tin.
- Combine brown sugar and cinnamon. Toss apple slices in combined ingredients. Set aside.
- Sift flour and baking powder together. Set aside.
- Beat sugar and eggs. Add corn oil and vanilla essence. Beat well. Sift in sifted ingredients. Add salt.
- Spread batter evenly in prepared tin. Bake for 15 minutes.
- Remove cake from oven. Quickly add cheese topping and arrange apple slices atop cheese. Return to oven for 35–40 minutes.

*Cheese Topping

INGREDIENTS:

Cream cheese	250 g, softened at room temperature
Sugar	55 g
Egg	1
Vanilla essence (extract)	1/2 tsp

METHOD:

- Beat cream cheese until smooth, then cream with sugar. When mixture is creamy, add egg and vanilla essence. Beat until smooth.

Preparation time: 15 minutes; Baking time: 60 minutes
Oven setting: 175°C, 350°F, Gas Regulo 6

INDONESIAN LAYER CAKE

Kek lapis is the name by which most people know this layer cake.

INGREDIENTS

Eggs	7, separated into yolks and whites
Sugar	150 g
Vanilla essence (extract)	1 tsp
Butter	150 g, softened at room temperature and beaten
Brandy	1 Tbsp
Plain (all-purpose) flour	90 g, sifted
Mixed spice	1/4 tsp, sifted

METHOD

- Grease base and sides of a 17-cm square cake tin. Line base with greased greaseproof paper.
- Whisk eggs yolks, sugar and vanilla essence until creamy. Beat in butter and brandy. Stir in sifted ingredients. Set aside.
- Whisk eggs whites until just stiff. Pour egg-yolk mixture over beaten egg whites. Fold gently.
- Place prepared tin under preheated grill for 1 minute. Remove from grill and add a ladleful of batter. Spread batter evenly by rolling wrist to tilt tin. Return to grill for 5 minutes or until lightly brown. Repeat until batter is used up.
- After last layer, turn out and leave to cool on a wire rack.

Apr 17/11

YOGHURT CAKE

INGREDIENTS

Cocoa (unsweetened)	2 Tbsp
Instant coffee	2 Tbsp
Water	115 ml, boiling
Bicarbonate of (baking) soda	2 tsp
Self-raising flour	300 g 2.5 c.
~~Salt~~	1/4 tsp
Corn oil	250 ml – 1c (some o.j.)
Sugar	340 g – 1.5c.
Eggs	4, large
Yoghurt	250 g – 1c
Vanilla essence (extract)	1 tsp

1c. self rising = 1c + 1½ t. BP + ½ t. salt

METHOD

- Line a 22-cm square cake tin with greased greaseproof paper.
- Dissolve cocoa and coffee in boiling water. Stir in bicarbonate of soda. Leave to cool.
- Sift flour onto a baking sheet and stir in salt.
- Beat corn oil and sugar well. Add eggs one at a time, beating well before each addition. Fold in sifted flour alternately with yoghurt. Stir in cooled cocoa mixture and vanilla essence.
- Pour batter into prepared tin. Bake for 35–40 minutes.
- When cooled, cake can be eaten plain or cut into two layers to sandwich some whipped cream.

Preparation time: 20 minutes; Baking time: 50 minutes
Oven setting: 165°C, 325°F, Gas Regulo 5

HONEY COFFEE CAKE

INGREDIENTS

Plain (all-purpose) flour	360 g
Baking powder	1 tsp
Bicarbonate of (baking) soda	1 tsp
Ground cinnamon	1 tsp
Salt	1/4 tsp
Instant coffee	2 Tbsp
Vanilla essence (extract)	1 tsp
Water	225 ml, hot
Corn oil	250 ml
Sugar	115 g
Honey	225 ml
Eggs	4, large, separated into yolks and whites
Chopped nuts	65 g

METHOD

- Line and grease a 21-cm square cake tin.
- Sift flour, baking powder, bicarbonate of soda and cinnamon together. Stir in salt. Set aside.
- Combine instant coffee, vanilla essence and hot water. Set aside.
- Cream corn oil, sugar and honey. Beat in egg yolks until creamy. Fold in sifted ingredients alternately with coffee mixture. Stir in chopped nuts.
- Whisk egg whites until just stiff. Fold into batter one-third at a time.
- Pour batter into prepared tin. Bake for 45–50 minutes. Transfer to a wire rack to cool. Serve in slices spread with butter.

Preparation time: 20 minutes; Baking time: 45 minutes
Oven setting: 165°C, 325°F, Gas Regulo 5

CARROT CAKE

INGREDIENTS

Castor (superfine) sugar	225 g
Corn oil	250 ml
Eggs	3, large
Plain (all-purpose) flour	150 g
Baking powder	1 1/2 tsp
Bicarbonate of (baking) soda	1 1/3 tsp
Ground cinnamon	1 1/3 tsp
Salt	1/2 tsp
Carrot	250 g, grated
Chopped nuts	125 g

METHOD

- Line a 22-cm square cake tin with greased greaseproof paper.
- Beat sugar in corn oil. Beat in eggs one at a time. Sift in dry ingredients. Add salt and fold into mixture. Stir in grated carrot and chopped nuts.
- Pour batter into prepared tin. Bake for about 45 minutes or until skewer inserted into cake's centre comes out clean.

Preparation time: 15 minutes; Cooking time: 10 minutes; Baking time: 15 minutes
Oven setting: 175°C, 350°F, Gas Regulo 6

PEACH CUSTARD SANDWICH CAKE

INGREDIENTS

Corn oil	1 Tbsp
Rum	1 Tbsp
Peach syrup	2 Tbsp
Eggs	4, large
Castor (superfine) sugar	115 g
Self-raising flour	120 g, sifted
Canned sliced peaches	1 can (870 g)
Custard cream*	1 recipe

METHOD

- Combine corn oil, rum and 1 Tbsp syrup. Set aside.
- Whisk eggs and sugar until light and fluffy. Sift in sifted flour. Fold quickly. Stir in corn-oil mixture.
- Line two 18 x 27-cm tins with greased greaseproof paper. Divide batter equally between tins. Bake for 10–15 minutes or until golden. Drizzle remaining syrup over cakes.
- Sandwich custard cream between cakes. Spread cream over top and sides of cake sandwich as desired. Arrange peach slices decoratively on cake. If preferred, cake can be served chilled.

*Custard Cream

INGREDIENTS:

Corn flour (cornstarch)	40 g
Custard powder	40 g
Milk (A)	115 ml
Milk (B)	450 ml
Sugar	115 g
Butter	45 g
Egg	1, well beaten
Vanilla essence (extract)	1 tsp
Peach syrup	1 Tbsp
Rum	1 Tbsp

METHOD:

- Blend corn flour, custard powder and milk (A). Set aside.
- Bring milk (B), sugar and butter to the boil in a saucepan. Add blended mixture, stirring constantly until mixture thickens. Remove from heat.
- Beat in egg, vanilla essence, peach syrup and rum.

Preparation time: 15 minutes; Baking time: 50 minutes
Oven setting: 165°C, 325°F, Gas Regulo 5

HONEY SOUR CREAM CAKE

INGREDIENTS

Plain (all-purpose) flour	300 g
Bicarbonate of (baking) soda	2 tsp
Baking powder	1/2 tsp
Ground cinnamon	1 tsp
Ground nutmeg	1 tsp
Salt	1/4 tsp
Corn oil	115 ml
Brown sugar	225 g
Eggs	4, large, separated into yolks and whites
Honey	175 ml
Sour cream	300 g
Chopped nuts	125 g

METHOD

- Line and grease the base of a 25–27-cm tube pan.
- Sift flour, bicarbonate of soda, baking powder, cinnamon and nutmeg together. Add salt. Set aside.
- Cream corn oil and sugar. Beat in egg yolks one at a time until light and creamy. Beat in honey. Fold in sifted ingredients alternately with sour cream. Stir in nuts.
- Beat egg whites until just stiff. Fold into batter one-third at a time.
- Pour batter into prepared tin. Bake for 45–50 minutes or until a skewer inserted into cake's centre comes out clean.

Preparation time: 20 minutes; Baking time: 45 minutes
Oven setting: 165°C, 325°F, Gas Regulo 5

ORANGE PRUNE CAKE

INGREDIENTS

Butter	250 g
Castor (superfine) sugar	210 g
Orange rind	grated from 2 oranges
Vanilla essence (extract)	1 tsp
Eggs	4, large
Self-raising flour	250 g, sifted
Water	3 Tbsp, lukewarm
Dried prunes	120 g, pitted and chopped

METHOD

- Line a 22-cm square cake tin with greased greaseproof paper.
- Cream butter and sugar until light and fluffy. Add orange rind and vanilla essence. Beat until well combined. Add eggs one at a time, beating well after each addition. Fold in flour a little at a time. Stir in water. Add chopped prunes.
- Pour batter into prepared tin. Bake on centre shelf for 45–50 minutes. The cake keeps well for 2–3 days in an airtight container.

Preparation time: 15 minutes; Baking time: 40 minutes
Oven setting: 175°C, 350°F, Gas Regulo 6

CRUNCHY-TOP CAKE

INGREDIENTS

Butter	250 g
Castor (superfine) sugar	210 g
Orange rind	grated from 1 orange
Lemon rind	grated from 1 lemon
Eggs	4, large
Self-raising flour	240 g
Orange juice or milk	1 Tbsp
Demerara (pale brown granulated) sugar	60 g

METHOD

- Line a 20-cm round cake tin with grease greaseproof paper.
- Cream butter and sugar until light and fluffy. Add orange and lemon rind. Add eggs one at a time, beating well after each addition. Sift in half the flour, then stir. Repeat with other half. Stir in orange juice or milk.
- Spoon batter into prepared tin. Even out surface. Bake on centre shelf for 25 minutes.
- Without removing cake from oven, sprinkle demerara sugar over the top. Bake for 15 minutes or until cake is done. To test, a skewer inserted into cake's centre should come out clean.

Preparation time: 20 minutes; Baking time: 50 minutes
Oven setting: 175°C, 350°F, Gas Regulo 6

SURPRISE CAKE

INGREDIENTS

Butter	250 g
Castor (superfine) sugar	210 g
Vanilla essence (extract)	1 tsp
Lemon essence (extract)	1 tsp
Eggs	3, large
Self-raising flour	240 g, sifted
Salt	1 pinch
Pineapple juice	2 Tbsp
Pineapple topping*	1 recipe

METHOD

- Line a 22-cm round cake tin with greaseproof paper.
- Cream butter and sugar until light and creamy. Add essences. Beat in eggs one at a time. Fold in sifted flour. Add salt. Mix in pineapple juice.
- Spoon half the batter into prepared tin. Spoon half the topping over batter and spread evenly. Repeat with other halves to form four alternating layers. Bake for 40–45 minutes or until cake is golden.
- Remove cake from oven and quickly spoon 2 Tbsp pineapple juice over the top. Switch oven setting to grill, then return cake to oven for 10–12 minutes or until topping turns light brown.

*Pineapple Topping

INGREDIENTS:

Butter	120 g
Brown sugar	115 g
Cornflakes	30 g, crushed
Canned pineapple	1 can (565 g), chopped
Desiccated coconut	30 g

METHOD:

- Cream butter and sugar. Add cornflakes, pineapple and coconut.

Preparation time: 15 minutes; Baking time: 30 minutes
Oven setting: 175°C, 350°F, Gas Regulo 6

COCONUT CAKE

INGREDIENTS

Butter	120 g
Castor (superfine) sugar	115 g
Eggs	2, large
Self-raising flour	150 g, sifted
Salt	1 pinch

Topping

Desiccated coconut	180 g
Castor (superfine) sugar	150 g
Eggs	2, large, beaten
Vanilla essence (extract)	1 tsp

METHOD

- Grease and line a 20-cm square cake tin with greased greaseproof paper.
- Cream butter and sugar until light and fluffy. Add eggs one at a time. Fold in sifted flour and salt. Spread batter evenly over tin's base.
- Combine all topping ingredients. Spread evenly over batter.
- Bake for 30–40 minutes.

Preparation time: 15 minutes; Cooking time: 10 minutes; Baking time: 40 minutes
Oven setting: 175°C, 350°F, Gas Regulo 6

WHISKY SPICE CAKE

INGREDIENTS

Raisins	180 g
Water	250 ml
Butter	250 g
Soft brown sugar	270 g
Eggs	3, large
Plain (all-purpose) flour	300 g
Bicarbonate of (baking) soda	2 tsp
Mixed spice	1 tsp
Ground nutmeg	1 tsp
Chopped nuts	65 g
Whisky	3 Tbsp

METHOD

- Grease and line a 22-cm square tin with greased greaseproof paper.
- Put raisins and water in a small saucepan. Simmer for 10 minutes. Drain raisins and reserve liquid.
- Cream butter and sugar until light and fluffy. Beat in eggs one at a time.
- Sift powdered ingredients over creamed mixture. Fold in with 3 Tbsp raisin liquid. Add nuts, raisins and whisky.
- Pour batter into prepared tin. Bake on centre shelf for 40–50 minutes .

Preparation time: 25 minutes; Baking time: 50 minutes
Oven setting: 175°C, 350°F, Gas Regulo 6

TEA CAKE

INGREDIENTS

Mixed fruit	250 g, chopped
Mixed peel	120 g, chopped
Strong tea	125 ml, cooled
Self-raising flour	240 g
Ground cinnamon	1 tsp
Ground nutmeg	1 tsp
Butter	180 g
Brown sugar	180 g
Orange rind	grated from 1–2 oranges
Eggs	2

METHOD

- Soak mixed fruit and peel in cooled strong tea overnight.
- On baking day, line a 20-cm square cake tin with greased greaseproof paper. Set aside.
- Sift flour, cinnamon and nutmeg together. Set aside.
- Beat butter and sugar until light and creamy. Add orange rind. Beat in eggs one at a time. Add tea-soaked ingredients. Fold in sifted ingredients.
- Spread batter evenly in prepared cake tin. Bake for 50 minutes or until a skewer inserted into cake's centre comes out clean.

Preparation time: 30 minutes; Baking time: 12 minutes
Oven setting: 190°C, 375°F, Gas Regulo 7

KALEIDOSCOPE CHEESECAKE

INGREDIENTS

Eggs	2, large
Castor (superfine) sugar	60 g
Vanilla essence (extract)	1/2 tsp
Self-raising flour	60 g, sifted
Corn oil	1/2 Tbsp
Pineapple syrup	1 Tbsp
Cheese topping*	1 recipe
Whipped cream (optional)	

METHOD

- Grease and flour a 21–22 cm round springform cake tin.
- Whisk eggs, sugar and vanilla essence until light and fluffy. Sift in flour. Fold quickly. Stir in corn oil and pineapple syrup.
- Bake for 10–12 minutes or until light brown. Leave to cool.
- Pour cheese topping onto cooled sponge base. Refrigerate until firm. Decorate with whipped cream if desired.

*Cheese Topping

INGREDIENTS:

Lemon jelly	45 g
Lime jelly	45 g
Cherry or strawberry jelly	45 g
Cream cheese	250 g, softened at room temperature
Gelatin	1 Tbsp, dissolved in 115 ml hot water and cooled
Castor (superfine) sugar	180 g
Vanilla essence (extract)	1 tsp
Orange juice	extracted from 2 oranges
Eggs whites	2

METHOD:

- Dissolve each jelly flavour in 115 ml hot water in separate small dishes. Let jelly set. Refrigerate overnight. Cut into 1-cm cubes.
- Blend (process) cream cheese, cooled gelatin, sugar, vanilla essence and orange juice until smooth.
- Whisk egg whites until just stiff. Fold into blended ingredients. Add jelly cubes.

Note:
Leftover cake must be refrigerated or jelly cubes will turn watery.

Preparation time: 15 minutes; Baking time: 12 minutes
Oven setting 190°C, 375°F, Gas Regulo 7

PINEAPPLE CHEESECAKE

INGREDIENTS

Eggs	2, large
Castor (superfine) sugar	60 g
Vanilla essence (extract)	1/2 tsp
Self-raising flour	60 g, sifted
Corn oil	1/2 Tbsp
Pineapple syrup	1 Tbsp
Cheese topping*	1 recipe
Whipped cream (optional)	

METHOD

- Grease and flour a 21-cm round springform cake tin.
- Whisk eggs, sugar and vanilla essence until light and fluffy. Sift in flour. Fold quickly. Stir in corn oil and pineapple syrup.
- Bake for 10–12 minutes or until light brown. Leave to cool.
- Pour cheese topping onto cooled sponge base. Refrigerate until firm. Decorate with whipped cream if desired.

*Cheese Topping

INGREDIENTS:

Cream cheese	250 g, softened at room temperature
Sugar	90 g
Gelatin	1 Tbsp, dissolved in 115 ml hot water and cooled
Vanilla essence (extract)	1 tsp
Pineapple syrup	115 ml
Egg whites	2
Pineapple rings	1 can (450 g), diced

METHOD:

- Blend (process) cream cheese, sugar, cooled gelatin, vanilla essence and pineapple syrup until smooth.
- Whisk egg whites until just stiff but not dry. Fold blended ingredients into beaten egg whites. Add pineapple pieces.

Preparation time: 25 minutes; Baking time: 25 minutes
Oven setting: 175°C, 350°F, Gas Regulo 6

DREAMY CHEESECAKE

INGREDIENTS

Butter	180 g
Icing (confectioners') sugar	150 g, sifted
Vanilla essence (extract)	1/2 tsp
Egg yolks	2
Egg white	1
Self-raising flour	150 g, sifted
Water	75 ml, cold
Cheese topping*	1 recipe
Melted chocolate (optional)	

METHOD

- Line base of 21–22-cm round springform cake tin with greased greaseproof paper.
- Cream butter and sugar until light and fluffy. Add vanilla essence. Beat in egg yolks one at a time, then egg white. Fold in sifted flour alternately with water. If necessary, add a little more water to achieve dropping consistency.
- Pour batter into prepared tin. Even out surface. Bake for 25–30 minutes.
- Remove cake from oven. Add cheese topping and spread evenly. Grill for about 10 minutes or until topping is firm to the touch. To prevent top surface from browning, cover with a flat tin lid.
- Top with melted chocolate if preferred.

*Cheese Topping

INGREDIENTS:

Cream cheese	250 g, softened at room temperature
Egg yolks	2
Castor (superfine) sugar	4 Tbsp
Vanilla essence (extract)	1 tsp
Lemon essence (extract)	1 tsp
Egg whites	4

METHOD:

- Beat cream cheese until smooth. Add egg yolks one at a time. Add sugar and essences.
- Whisk egg whites until soft peaks form. Fold lightly into cream-cheese mixture.

Preparation time: 15 minutes; Baking time: 40 minutes
Oven setting: 175°C, 350°F, Gas Regulo 6

HONEY CAKE

INGREDIENTS

Honey	60 ml
Water	1 Tbsp, hot
Self-raising flour	150 g
Bicarbonate of (baking) soda	1 tsp
Ground cinnamon	$^1/_2$ tsp
Corn oil	115 ml
Brown sugar	115 g
Eggs	3, large, separated into yolks and whites
Salt	1 pinch
Milk	1 Tbsp

METHOD

- Line a 17-cm square cake tin with greased greaseproof paper.
- Dissolve honey in hot water. Set aside.
- Sift flour, bicarbonate of soda and cinnamon together, twice. Set aside.
- Beat corn oil and sugar. Add egg yolks one at a time. Beat in honey mixture. Add salt. Fold in sifted ingredients. Stir in milk.
- Whisk egg whites until stiff. Pour egg-yolk mixture over beaten egg whites. Fold carefully.
- Pour batter into prepared tin. Bake for 35–40 minutes or until well-risen and cooked through. To test, a skewer inserted into cake's centre should come out clean.

Preparation time: 30 minutes; Baking time: 50 minutes
Oven setting: 175°C, 350°F, Gas Regulo 6

FRUITY FRUITSIE CAKE

INGREDIENTS

Raisins	360 g
Currants	240 g
Glacé (candied) cherries	120 g, quartered
Chopped nuts	120 g
Mixed peel	120 g, cut into smaller pieces
Soft brown sugar (A)	1 Tbsp
Rum	6–8 Tbsp
Plain (all-purpose) flour	300 g
Baking powder	1 tsp
Mixed spice	1 tsp
Ground nutmeg	1 tsp
Butter	250 g
Soft brown sugar (B)	240 g
Eggs	6
Salt	1/4 tsp

METHOD

- Combine fruits, nuts, mixed peel, brown sugar (A) and 4–5 Tbsp rum in an airtight container. Leave to soak for at least 12 hours.
- On baking day, grease a 22–25-cm square tin and line with two layers of greaseproof paper. Grease top layer and set aside.
- Sift flour, baking powder, mixed spice and nutmeg together. Set aside.
- Cream butter and sugar until light. Beat in eggs one at a time. Stir in rum-soaked ingredients. Add sifted ingredients and salt.
- Pour batter into prepared tin. Bake for 50–60 minutes or until a skewer inserted into cake's centre comes out clean. Spoon 2–3 Tbsp rum over cake's top while still warm. Set aside until cold.
- Turn out cake without removing paper. Wrap in foil or store in polythene bag for one day before cutting. Cake keeps

Preparation time: 40 minutes; Cooking time: 5 minutes; Baking time: 15 minutes
Oven setting: 190°C, 375°F, Gas Regulo 7

LAYER DELIGHT

INGREDIENTS

Eggs	4, large
Castor (superfine) sugar	90 g
Vanilla essence (extract)	1 tsp
Self-raising flour	120 g, sifted
Corn oil	1 Tbsp
Milk	1 Tbsp
Rum	1–2 Tbsp
Rum cream*	1 recipe

METHOD

- Grease and flour two 20-cm round cake tins.
- Whisk eggs, sugar and vanilla essence until light and fluffy. Sift in sifted flour. Fold quickly. Stir in corn oil and milk.
- Divide mixture equally between two tins. Bake for 15 minutes.
- Remove from oven. Carefully spoon rum over cakes while still hot. Leave to cool on wire rack.
- Sandwich rum cream (with raisins) between cakes. Coat and pipe top and sides with remaining cream (without raisins).

*Rum Cream

INGREDIENTS:

Seedless raisins	180 g
Rum	4 Tbsp
Butter	250 g, cold and cut into small cubes
Icing (confectioners') sugar	150 g, sifted
Vanilla essence (extract)	1 tsp
Evaporated milk	1 small can (170 g), chilled

METHOD:

- Put raisins and 3 Tbsp rum into a small saucepan. Bring to the boil over low heat. Leave to cool.
- Cream butter pieces and sugar until light and creamy. Add vanilla essence. Beat in milk a little at a time. Beat in remaining rum.
- Halve cream mixture. Add raisins to only one portion.

Preparation time: 15 minutes; Cooking time: 30 minutes; Baking time: 15 minutes
Oven setting: 190°C, 375°F, Gas Regulo 7

PAPAYA SPONGE FLAN

INGREDIENTS

Corn flour (cornstarch)	45 g
Plain (all-purpose) flour	15 g
Baking powder	$^3/_4$ tsp
Eggs	2
Castor (superfine) sugar	55 g
Lemon essence (extract)	$^1/_2$ tsp
Corn oil	1 Tbsp
Milk	2 tsp
Papaya topping*	1 recipe

METHOD

- Grease a 21-cm round springform cake tin.
- Sift flours and baking powder together. Set aside.
- Whisk eggs, sugar and lemon essence until light and fluffy. Sift in sifted ingredients. Fold though quickly and evenly. Stir in corn oil and milk.
- Pour batter into prepared tin. Bake for 10–15 minutes or until cake springs back when lightly touched with a finger.
- Pour papaya topping onto cooled cake. Refrigerate until firm.

*Papaya Topping

INGREDIENTS:

Papaya	1, 1–1.5 kg and ripe
Orange rind	grated from 1 orange
Sugar	115 g
Lemon essence (extract)	1 tsp
Vanilla essence (extract)	1 tsp
Gelatin	2 Tbsp
Water	115 ml, hot
Cream	1 small can (170 g)

METHOD:

- Skin papaya and remove seeds. Cut into cubes.
- Blend (process) papaya and orange rind. Pour blended ingredients into a saucepan. Cover and cook over medium heat, stirring occasionally.
- When papaya pulp is reduced to about 2$^1/_2$–3 cups, remove from heat. Leave to cool.
- Stir in sugar and essences. Add gelatin dissolved in hot water. Set aside.
- Whisk cream until firm peaks form. Fold lightly into papaya mixture.

Preparation time: 20 minutes; Cooking time: 15 minutes; Baking time: 15 minutes
Oven Setting: 190°C, 375°F, Gas Regulo 7

FAMILY FAVOURITE CUSTARD FLAN

INGREDIENTS

Plain (all-purpose) flour	45 g
Corn flour (cornstarch)	15 g
Baking powder	3/4 tsp
Eggs	2, large
Castor (superfine) sugar	55 g
Vanilla essence (extract)	1/2 tsp
Corn oil	1/2 Tbsp
Coconut cream	1 Tbsp
Custard topping*	1 recipe
Chocolate rice	

METHOD

- Grease and flour a 21-cm round spring cake tin.
- Sift flours and baking powder together. Set aside.
- Whisk eggs, sugar and vanilla essence until light and fluffy. Sift in sifted ingredients. Fold quickly. Stir in corn oil and coconut cream.
- Pour batter into prepared tin. Even out surface. Bake for 15 minutes or until well risen and light brown. Leave to cool in tin.
- Pour custard topping over cooled cake. When custard cools, sprinkle a little chocolate rice over the top. Serve chilled.

*Custard Topping

INGREDIENTS:

Custard powder	30 g
Coconut cream	225 ml, squeezed from 1/2 grated coconut and sufficient water
Coconut milk	340 ml, squeezed from same 1/2 grated coconut and sufficient water
Sugar	75 g
Salt	1 pinch
Vanilla essence (extract)	1/2 tsp

METHOD:

- Dissolve custard powder in a little coconut milk. Transfer to a saucepan. Add remaining coconut milk, sugar and salt. Stir over low heat.
- When mixture is near boiling, add coconut cream and vanilla essence. Keep stirring until mixture comes to a bubbly boil.

Note:
Coconut cream, or thick coconut milk, is the liquid produced by pressing or squeezing grated coconut for the first time, sometimes with water added. Coconut milk, or thin coconut milk, is the liquid produced by second and subsequent pressings, often with water added.

Preparation time: 15 minutes; Baking time: 35 minutes
Oven setting: 175°C, 350°F, Gas Regulo 6

COFFEE CAKE

INGREDIENTS

Self-raising flour	120 g
Plain (all-purpose) flour	60 g
Bicarbonate of (baking) soda	1 tsp
Instant coffee	3 tsp
Milk	1 Tbsp
Corn oil	250 ml
Sugar	170 g
Eggs	3
Coffee topping*	1 recipe

METHOD

- Line a 22-cm square cake tin with greased greaseproof paper.
- Sift flours and bicarbonate of soda together. Set aside.
- Dissolve instant coffee in milk. Set aside.
- Beat corn oil and sugar. Add eggs one at a time. Fold in sifted ingredients. Stir in coffee mixture.
- Pour batter into prepared tin. Bake for 25 minutes.
- Remove cake from oven. Quickly spread topping on surface. Return to oven for 10–15 minutes or until topping bubbles and turns dark brown.

*Coffee Topping

INGREDIENTS:

Butter	45 g
Brown sugar	2 Tbsp
Instant coffee	1 Tbsp

METHOD:

- Cream butter and sugar. Stir in instant coffee.

Preparation time: 15 minutes; Cooking time: 15 minutes; Baking time: 15 minutes
Oven setting: 190°C, 375°F, Gas Regulo 7

AGAR-AGAR FLAN DELIGHT

INGREDIENTS

Eggs	2, large
Castor (superfine) sugar	55 g
Vanilla essence (extract)	1/2 tsp
Self-raising flour	60 g
Corn oil	1/2 Tbsp
Milk	1/2 Tbsp
Agar-agar topping*	1 recipe
Glacé (candied) cherries	2–3

METHOD

- Grease a 20–22-cm flan tin.
- Whisk eggs, sugar and vanilla essence until thick and white. Sift in flour. Fold quickly. Stir in corn oil and milk.
- Bake for 15 minutes or until golden. Let cake cool before turning out.
- Pour agar-agar topping onto cooled cake. When topping cools, decorate with cherries. Refrigerate.

*Agar-agar topping

INGREDIENTS:

Agar-agar strips	7 g
Water	340 ml
Sugar	115 g
Vanilla essence (extract)	1 tsp
Red food colouring	2–3 drops
Egg white	1, large

METHOD:

- Wash agar-agar strips, then boil in water. Add sugar and stir to dissolve. Remove from heat. Add vanilla essence and food colouring.
- Beat egg white until just stiff. Strain jelly mixture into egg white, whisking at the same time.

Preparation time: 15 minutes; Baking time: 12–15 minutes
Oven setting: 190°C, 375°F, Gas Regulo 7

CINNAMON ROLL

INGREDIENTS

Corn flour (cornstarch)	60 g
Plain (all-purpose) flour	30 g
Baking powder	2 tsp
Ground cinnamon	2 tsp
Eggs	3
Castor (superfine) sugar	90 g
Vanilla essence (extract)	1 tsp
Honey spread*	1 recipe; replaceable with whipped cream

METHOD

- Line a Swiss roll tin (approx. 27 x 27-cm) with greased greaseproof paper.
- Sift flours, baking powder and cinnamon together. Set aside.
- Whisk eggs until light and fluffy. Gradually beat in sugar. Add vanilla essence. Sift in sifted ingredients. Fold carefully.
- Spread batter evenly in prepared tin. Bake for 12–15 minutes until golden brown and springy to the touch.
- Turn out onto a tea towel. Peel off paper. Trim off crisp edges. Gently roll up.
- When cold, gently unroll. Spread with honey spread or whipped cream and roll up.

*Honey Spread

INGREDIENTS:

Butter	90 g
Honey	3 Tbsp

METHOD:

- Beat butter until light. Add honey, 1 Tbsp at a time

Preparation time: 45 minutes; Baking time: 25 minutes
Oven setting: 175°C, 350°F, Gas Regulo 6

COFFEE BRANDY SPONGE

INGREDIENTS

Corn flour (cornstarch)	60 g
Plain (all-purpose) flour	60 g
Baking powder	2 tsp
Instant coffee	2 tsp
Water	2 tsp
Brandy	1 Tbsp
Eggs	4
Castor (superfine) sugar	115 g
Corn oil	2 Tbsp
Coffee cream*	1 recipe

METHOD

- Line two 21-cm round cake tins with greased greaseproof paper.
- Sift flours and baking powder together. Set aside.
- Combine coffee, water and brandy. Set aside.
- Whisk eggs and sugar until light and fluffy. Sift in sifted ingredients a little at a time. Quickly but carefully fold into egg mixture. Add corn oil and coffee mixture.
- Divide batter equally between prepared tins. Bake for 25 minutes or until cakes are springy to the touch.
- When cool, horizontally slice one cake into two. Sandwich coffee cream between slices. Repeat with second cake.
- Spread cream on top surface of one cake sandwich. Secure base of other cake sandwich over cream, forming a stack of four. Coat and pipe top and sides with remaining cream.

*Coffee Cream

INGREDIENTS:

Instant coffee	2 tsp
Brandy	1 Tbsp
Butter	250 g, cold and in small pieces
Icing (confectioners') sugar	150 g, sifted
Vanilla essence (extract)	1 tsp
Evaporated milk	1 small can (170 g), chilled

METHOD:

- Combine coffee and brandy. Set aside.
- Cream butter pieces and sugar until creamy. Add vanilla essence. Beat in cold milk a little at a time. Add coffee-and-brandy mixture.

Preparation time: 15 minutes; Baking time: 45 minutes
Oven setting: 175°C, 350°F, Gas Regulo 6

BANANA HONEY-TOP CAKE

INGREDIENTS

Butter	250 g
Castor (superfine) sugar	170 g
Vanilla essence (extract)	1/2 tsp
Eggs	4, large
Small ripe bananas (*pisang rastali*)	4 medium or 5 small, finely mashed with a fork
Self-raising flour	240 g
Milk	1 Tbsp
Honey topping*	1 recipe

METHOD

- Line a 22-cm round cake tin with greased greaseproof paper.
- Cream butter, sugar and vanilla essence until light and fluffy. Beat in eggs one at a time. Add mashed bananas. Sift in half the flour. Carefully fold into mixture. Repeat with other half. Stir in milk to achieve soft, dropping consistency.
- Pour batter into prepared tin. Bake for 35 minutes.
- Remove cake from oven. Quickly spread honey topping on surface. Return to oven for 10 minutes or until topping is set.

*Honey Topping

INGREDIENTS:

Butter	45 g
Honey	1 Tbsp
Brown sugar	45 g
Ground cinnamon	1/2 tsp
Rum or brandy (optional)	1 tsp

METHOD:

- Cream butter, honey and sugar. Add cinnamon, then rum or brandy if used.

cookies

Preparation time: 40 minutes; Baking time: 15 minutes
Oven setting: 175°C, 350°F, Gas Regulo 6; Makes: 50

SESAME COOKIES

INGREDIENTS

Plain (all-purpose) flour	120 g
Self-raising flour	120 g
Vegetable shortening	180 g
Castor (superfine) sugar	170 g
Egg yolk	1
Salt	1/4 tsp
Lemon essence (extract)	1 tsp
Milk	1 Tbsp
Sesame seeds	175 g, washed and oven-toasted

METHOD

- Sift flours together. Set aside.
- Cream vegetable shortening and sugar. Beat in egg yolk until creamy. Add salt and lemon essence. Gradually fold in sifted ingredients. Stir in milk.
- Shape teaspoonfuls of the mixture into balls. Roll balls in sesame seeds. Place on greased trays.
- Bake for 15–20 minutes.

Preparation time: 30 minutes; Baking time: 15 minutes
Oven setting: 175°C, 350°F, Gas Regulo 6; Makes: 62

CASHEW NUT ROUNDS

INGREDIENTS

Self-raising flour	150 g
Plain (all-purpose) flour	120 g
Butter	120 g
Vegetable shortening	120 g
Sugar	115 g
Vanilla essence (extract)	1 tsp
Salt	1 pinch
Ground cashew nuts	150 g
Glacé (candied) cherries	16–20, quartered

METHOD

- Sift flours together. Set aside.
- Cream butter, vegetable shortening and sugar until smooth. Add vanilla essence and salt. Stir in cashew nuts and sifted ingredients. Mix well.
- Shape teaspoonfuls of the mixture into balls. Press a cherry quarter into the centre of each ball. Place on ungreased trays.
- Bake for 15 minutes until light golden. Leave to cool on trays.

Preparation time: 30 minutes; Baking time: 20 minutes
Oven setting: 175°C, 350°F, Gas Regulo 6; Makes: 20

NUTTY CRISPS

INGREDIENTS

Orange juice	1 tsp
Egg yolk	1/2
Plain (all-purpose) flour	120 g
Corn flour (cornstarch)	60 g
Butter	120 g, cold and cut into small cubes
Sugar	90 g
Egg white	1/2, lightly beaten
Chopped nuts	75 g

METHOD

- Combine orange juice and egg yolk. Set aside.
- Sift flours into a mixing bowl. Add butter pieces. Blend with a pastry cutter or knife. Stir in sugar. Bind dough with orange-juice mixture.
- On a lightly floured board, roll dough into a thin sheet. Cut 6-cm circles.
- Transfer cookies onto greased baking trays, lifting with a flat, broad-bladed knife. Brush with egg white. Sprinkle nuts over the top.
- Bake for 20 minutes or until golden brown. Remove and leave to cool. Store in airtight containers.

Preparation time: 30 minutes; Baking time: 15 minutes
Oven setting: 175°C, 350°F, Gas Regulo 6; Makes: 52

CHOCOLATE CRINKLES

INGREDIENTS

Plain (all-purpose) flour	240 g
Baking powder	1 tsp
Cocoa (unsweetened)	30 g
Butter	180 g
Icing (confectioners') sugar	180 g
Egg yolks	2
Raisins	120 g, chopped
Chopped nuts	60 g
Salt	1 pinch

METHOD

- Sift flour, baking powder and cocoa together. Set aside.
- Cream butter and sugar. Beat in egg yolks. Stir in raisins and nuts. Gradually fold in sifted ingredients and salt.
- Shape into small balls. Place on greased trays.
- Bake for 15 minutes. When done, transfer to a wire rack to cool. Store in airtight containers when completely cold.

Preparation time: 60 minutes; Baking time: 20 minutes
Oven setting: 175°C, 350°F, Gas Regulo 6; Makes: 24 pairs

NUT FINGERS

INGREDIENTS

Plain (all-purpose) flour	210 g
Baking powder	2 tsp
Castor (superfine) sugar	90 g
Vanilla essence (extract)	3/4 tsp
Salt	1 pinch
Egg yolk	1
Egg white	1, halved
Butter	105 g, cold and cut into small cubes
Peanuts (groundnuts)	
Favourite jam	

METHOD

- Sift flour and baking powder into a mixing bowl. Add sugar, vanilla essence, salt, egg yolk and 1/2 egg white. Stir to mix well.
- Add butter pieces. Blend with pastry cutter or knife. Work with fingers to form a ball of soft dough.
- On a floured board, roll dough into a 3-mm thick rectangle. Cut 10 x 1-cm fingers.
- Carefully transfer fingers onto well-greased trays, lifting with a flat, broad-bladed knife. Brush with remaining egg white. Decorate with peanuts.
- Bake for 20 minutes or until golden brown. Remove and leave to cool.
- Sandwich jam between two fingers. Store in airtight containers.

Preparation time: 40 minutes; Baking time: 20 minutes
Oven setting: 175°C, 350°F, Gas Regulo 6; Makes: 22

RAINBOW WHEELS

INGREDIENTS

Self-raising flour	180 g
Salt	1 pinch
Vegetable shortening	45 g
Butter	45 g
Castor (superfine) sugar	90 g
Vanilla essence (extract)	1 tsp
Egg	1, beaten
Green food colouring	a few drops
Orange food colouring	a few drops

METHOD

- Sift flour into a mixing bowl. Add salt. Rub in vegetable shortening and butter. Stir in sugar and vanilla essence. Bind mixture with beaten egg.
- Divide dough into 3 equal portions. Colour one portion green and one orange; leave the third uncoloured.
- Place each portion between lightly floured plastic sheets. Roll into 15 x 22.5-cm rectangles.
- Remove plastic sheets to stack one rectangle on top of another, with the uncoloured rectangle in the centre.
- Roll into tight Swiss roll. Freeze for 10–15 minutes. Remove from freezer. Cut 0.5-cm thick slices.
- Place apart on greased trays. Bake for 15–20 minutes until light golden.

Preparation time: 30 minutes; Baking time: 15 minutes
Oven setting: 175°C, 350°F, Gas Regulo 6; Makes: 50

CUSTARD CRISPS

INGREDIENTS

Plain (all-purpose) flour	180 g
Custard powder	150 g
Baking powder	1/2 tsp
Butter	180 g
Icing (confectioners') sugar	120 g
Castor (superfine) sugar	1 Tbsp
Egg	1

METHOD

- Sift flour, custard and baking powders together. Set aside.
- Cream butter and sugars until light and fluffy. Beat in egg. Stir in sifted ingredients. Mix well.
- With lightly floured hands, shape teaspoonfuls of the mixture into balls. Place on lightly greased cookie trays.
- Dip a fork in flour, then lightly press down on the centre of each ball. Bake for 15 minutes.

Preparation time: 45 minutes; Baking time: 12 minutes
Oven setting: 190°C, 375°F, Gas Regulo 7; Makes: 36

CHEESE TWISTS

INGREDIENTS

Plain (all-purpose) flour	240 g
Baking powder	1 tsp
Pepper	1 dash
Salt	1 pinch
Butter	90 g
Chedder cheese	60 g, grated
Egg	1, beaten
Milk	2–4 tsp, cold

METHOD

- Sift flour and baking powder into a mixing bowl. Add pepper and salt. Either rub in butter with fingers or blend with a pastry cutter until mixture resembles breadcrumbs.
- Stir in cheese. Add egg. Mix with milk to form soft dough.
- On a lightly floured board, roll dough to 3-mm thickness. Cut 11 x 1-cm strips.
- Hold each strip, one hand at each end, and twist by turning ends in opposite directions. Place on lightly greased trays.
- Bake 12–15 minutes until golden. Transfer to a wire rack to cool.

Preparation time: 30 minutes; Baking time: 12 minutes
Oven setting: 175°C, 350°F, Gas Regulo 6; Makes: 34

CORNFLAKE CRUNCHIES

INGREDIENTS

Butter	105 g
Sugar	115 g
Egg yolk	1
Self-raising flour	90 g
Plain (all-purpose) flour	30 g
Raisins	100 g
Cornflakes	

METHOD

- Cream butter and sugar until light and fluffy. Beat in egg yolk. Sift in flours. Mix well. Stir in raisins.
- Roll teaspoonfuls of the mixture in lightly crushed cornflakes. Place on greased oven trays.
- Bake for 12–15 minutes.

Preparation time: 45 minutes; Baking time: 12 minutes
Oven setting: 175°C, 350°F, Gas Regulo 6; Makes: 42

CHEESE ROPES

INGREDIENTS

Butter	60 g
Cream cheese	60 g, softened at room temperature
Egg	1
Salt	1/2 tsp
Pepper	1 dash
Plain (all-purpose) flour	180 g
Baking powder	1 tsp

METHOD

- Cream butter and cheese. Beat in egg. Add salt and pepper. Sift in flour and baking powder. Mix to form soft dough.
- On a lightly floured board, roll out dough. Cut 1-cm wide strips.
- Shape each strip into a long and thin roll, then cut 12–13-cm lengths.
- Hold two lengths together, one hand at each end. Twist by turning ends in opposite directions. Place on ungreased trays. At each end, lightly press against tray to prevent unwinding.
- Bake for 12–15 minutes or until golden. Transfer to a wire rack to cool.

MURUKU

INGREDIENTS

Rice flour	480 g, sifted
Cumin	1 tsp
Ajowan	1 tsp
Salt	1 1/2 tsp
Baking powder	1 tsp
Butter	30 g, softened at room temperature
Coconut milk	675–900 ml, squeezed from 1 grated coconut and sufficient water
Cooking oil for deep-frying	

METHOD

- Roast rice flour in a wok over low heat for 5 minutes, stirring constantly. Take care not to brown flour. Remove from heat
  and leave to cool completely, preferably overnight.
- Add cumin, ajowan, salt and baking powder to flour. Add butter last. Gradually pour in enough coconut milk to form stiff dough.
- Heat oil in a wok. Put dough in a cookie press fitted with either a one- or a three-star nozzle. Pipe 7–8-cm lengths into hot oil.
- Fry over medium heat until golden brown. Drain on absorbent paper. When cool, store in airtight containers.

Preparation time: 30 minutes; Baking time: 8 minutes
Oven setting: 175°C, 350°F, Gas Regulo 6; Makes: 80

ORANGE BISCUITS

INGREDIENTS

Self-raising flour	120 g
Plain (all-purpose) flour	30 g
Rice flour	30 g
Butter	120 g
Castor (superfine) sugar	120 g
Orange rind	grated from 1 orange
Salt	1 pinch
Egg yolk	1
Orange juice	1 Tbsp

METHOD

- Sift flours together. Set aside.
- Cream butter and sugar until creamy. Add orange rind and salt.
- Sift in sifted ingredients. Fold into creamed mixture. Bind with egg yolk and orange juice.
- Put mixture into a cookie press. Pipe onto greased trays.
- Bake for 5–8 minutes or until light golden.

specially for children

Preparation time: 45 minutes; Baking time: 12 minutes
Oven setting: 190°C, 375°F, Gas Regulo 7; Makes: 30

BO PEEP'S COOKIE STAFFS

INGREDIENTS

Butter	120 g
Brown sugar	120 g
Vanilla essence (extract)	1/2 tsp
Salt	1 pinch
Egg	1
Plain (all-purpose) flour	240 g
Baking powder	1 tsp
Milk	4 tsp, cold
Egg white	1/2, beaten
Hundreds and thousands	

METHOD

- Cream butter and sugar until creamy. Add vanilla essence and salt. Beat in egg. Sift in flour and baking powder. Mix with milk to form soft dough.
- On a lightly floured board, roll tablespoonfuls of mixture into pencil-like sticks. Cut 12–15-cm lengths. Bend one end of each length to resemble the crook of a cane.
- Place on greased baking trays. Bush with egg white. Sprinkle hundreds and thousands over the top.
- Bake for 12–15 minutes until light brown. Carefully transfer to a wire rack to cool.

Preparation time: 15 minutes; Cooking time: 30 minutes
Makes: 30

COCONUT CANDY

INGREDIENTS

Grated skinned coconut	300 g
Sugar	565 g
Evaporated milk	1 small can (170 g)
Butter	45 g
Vanilla essence (extract)	1 tsp
Green food colouring	a few drops

METHOD

- Put coconut, sugar and milk into a heavy saucepan. Stir continuously over heat until sugar dissolves. Then, stir in butter, vanilla essence and food colouring. Keep stirring until mixture thickens. To test, bits of thickened mixture should form soft balls when dropped into a cup of cold water.
- Press suitably thickened mixture into a greased tray, approximately 15 x 18 cm. Cover with a plastic sheet. Use a rolling pin to even out surface. Leave to set and cool.
- When slightly cool, cut into squares. When completely cooled to room temperature, store in airtight containers.

WATERMELON JELLY

INGREDIENTS

Agar-agar strips	$1^1/_2$ packets (50 g)
Water	900 ml
Sugar	340 g
Skinned coconut	1, grated
Screwpine (*pandan*) leaves	3–4
Egg whites	7 large–8 medium
Red food colouring	a few drops
Black jelly (*chin chow*)	60 g, diced
Green food colouring	a few drops

METHOD

- Wash agar-agar strips. Put strips into a saucepan. Add water and sugar. Bring to the boil.
- While waiting for sugar to dissolve, squeeze grated coconut, without adding water, to obtain coconut cream. Strain.
- When sugar has dissolved, add screwpine leaves and coconut cream. Bring to the boil and remove from heat. Strain melted agar-agar into a measuring jug. About 900 ml of liquid should result.
- Whisk egg whites until just stiff. Whisk agar-agar liquid into egg whites until well combined. Pour into one 3-litre, 21-cm bowl or two 18-cm soup bowls.
- When top of jelly sets, use a small knife to cut a circle on the surface, about 2.5 cm from the edge. Add red colouring to the centre. Carefully mix with fingers, breaking lumps to get an even pink colour. Stir in black jelly to represent melon seeds. Refrigerate jelly and leave to set.
- Remove jelly from refrigerator. Invert onto a dish. Rub green colouring onto curved surface to represent melon skin. Refrigerate.

Preparation time: 15 minutes; Baking time: 90 minutes
Oven setting: 110°C, 225°F, Gas Regulo 1; Makes: 24

MERINGUE DROPS

INGREDIENTS

Icing (confectioners') sugar	60 g
Castor (superfine) sugar	60 g
Eggs whites	2
Vanilla essence (extract)	1/2 tsp
Glacé icing*	1 recipe
Confetti sprinkles	
Snowflake sprinkles	

METHOD

- Combine icing and castor sugars.
- Line a cookie tray with greased greaseproof paper.
- Whisk egg whites and vanilla essence until stiff. Gradually beat in half the sugar. Repeat with other half.
- Drop teaspoonfuls of meringue onto prepared tray. Bake for 90 minutes until firm.
- When cool, decorate as desired with such items as glacé icing and sprinkles.

*Glacé Icing

INGREDIENTS:

Icing (confectioners') sugar	120 g, sifted
Water	1 Tbsp, hot
Vanilla essence (extract)	2 drops

METHOD:

- Sift sugar into a bowl. Add water and vanilla essence. Mix well.

Preparation time: 30 minutes; Cooking time: 45 minutes
Makes: 24

KUIH SERIMUKA

INGREDIENTS

Skinned coconut	1/2, grated
Water	340 ml
Glutinous rice	450 g
Salt	1 1/4 tsp
Topping*	1 recipe

METHOD

- Combine coconut and water. Squeeze to obtain coconut milk. Strain.
- Wash glutinous rice. Put in a 25–27-cm round pan. Pour in enough coconut milk to cover rice. Stir in salt. Steam for 20–25 minutes.
- When cooked, firmly press down with the back of a spoon. Pour on topping. Steam for 20 minutes over medium heat.

*Topping

INGREDIENTS:

Skinned coconut	1, small, grated
Water	225 ml
Eggs	4
Sugar	180 g
Plain (all-purpose) flour	90 g
Tapioca flour	30 g
Screwpine (*pandan*) juice	55 ml, from pounding and squeezing screwpipe leaves
Green food colouring	a few drops
Vanilla essence (extract)	1/2 tsp

METHOD:

- Combine coconut and water. Squeeze to obtain about 340 ml coconut cream. Strain.
- Do not beat, but stir eggs and sugar together in a bowl. Sift in flours. Mix well.
- Gradually pour in coconut cream, screwpine juice, food colouring and vanilla essence. Strain to remove lumps.

pastries

Preparation time: 60 minutes; Baking time: 15 minutes
Oven setting: 205°C, 400°F, Gas Regulo 8; Makes: 16

RAISIN PINWHEELS

INGREDIENTS

Sugar	3 tsp
Milk	5 Tbsp, warm
Fresh yeast	30 g
Plain (all-purpose) flour	240 g, sifted
Salt	1 pinch
Butter	30 g, softened, or 30 ml corn oil
Egg	1, beaten
Raisins	60–90 g
Rum filling*	1 recipe

METHOD

- Dissolve sugar in milk. Drop in yeast. Let stand for 15 minutes until frothy.
- Sift flour into a bowl. Add salt. Mix in butter or corn oil. Add yeast liquid and egg. Beat with a wooden spoon. Cover with a damp cloth. Let stand for 60 minutes until dough doubles in volume.
- On a floured board, roll dough into a 20 x 25-cm rectangle. Fold evenly into three layers. Repeat process of rolling and folding. Halve dough.
- Roll each half into a 25 x 35-cm rectangle. Spread on rum filling and sprinkle on raisins. Roll up Swiss-roll style. Cut 2-cm wide slices using a flat-bladed knife.
- Place on greased baking trays. Leave for 15 minutes to rise. Bake for 12–15 minutes until golden. Transfer to a wire rack to cool.

*Rum Filling

INGREDIENTS:

Butter	60 g
Icing (confectioners') sugar	90 g, sifted
Rum	1 Tbsp

METHOD:

- Cream butter and sugar. Add rum.

Preparation time: 90 minutes; Cooking time: 30 minutes; Baking time: 20 minutes
Oven setting: 220°C, 425°F, Gas Regulo 9; Makes: 24

CHICKEN PIES

INGREDIENTS

Pastry margarine	180 g, at room temperature
Kalamansi lime juice	from 2 limes
Water	175 ml, cold
Salt	1/4 tsp
Egg yolk	1, beaten
Water	1 tsp
Plain (all-purpose) flour	480 g
Baking powder	1 1/2 tsp
Corn oil	90 ml, replaceable with cold butter
Egg	1, beaten
Filling*	1 recipe

METHOD

- Between large, clean plastic sheets, roll pastry margarine into a 20 x 15-cm rectangle. Refrigerate.
- Combine lime juice, water and salt. Set aside.
- Beat egg yolk and water together to make glaze.
- Sift flour and baking powder into a mixing bowl. Add corn oil or butter. Blend with pastry cutter or knife until mixture resembles breadcrumbs. Bind with beaten egg and lime-juice mixture using a wooden spoon.
- On a lightly floured board, knead bowl's contents. Resulting dough should be soft but not sticky.
- Roll dough into a rectangle that has the width of margarine rectangle but twice the length; or 40 x 15-cm.
- Remove plastic sheets from margarine. Place in centre of rolled out dough. Fold over ends of dough to cover margarine. Seal edge.
- Roll sealed parcel into a rectangle twice as long as it is wide. Fold rectangle into thirds widthways (widthwise). Repeat process of rolling and folding twice. Halve dough for easier handling. Use as required.
- On a lightly floured board, roll dough into a thin sheet. Cut 8.5-cm rounds with a plain cutter. Use rounds to line bases of patty tins. Cut 7.5-cm rounds with a fluted cutter for lids.
- Fill cavities with heaped teaspoonfuls of filling. Moisten rim of base pastry. Place lid on top. Press edges together. Prick top surface. Brush with glaze.
- Bake for 20 minutes or until golden.

*Filling

INGREDIENTS:

Light soy sauce	2 tsp
Sesame seed oil	1 tsp
Sugar	1 tsp
Salt	1/2 tsp
Pepper	1 dash
Chicken	240 g, diced
Cooking oil	1 Tbsp
Carrots	60 g, peeled and diced
Potatoes	120 g, peeled and diced
Onions	120 g, peeled and diced
Green peas	90 g
Corn flour (cornstarch)	1 tsp, mixed with 1 Tbsp water to make thickener
Spring onion (scallion)	1 stalk, chopped
Coriander (cilantro) leaves	1 sprig, chopped

METHOD:

- Combine light soy sauce, sesame seed oil, sugar, salt and pepper. Season chicken with combined ingredients.
- Heat 1/2 Tbsp oil in a wok. Lightly fry carrots and potatoes. Dish out. Set aside.
- Heat remaining oil. Fry 1 tsp onions until fragrant. Add seasoned chicken. When cooked, add fried carrots and potatoes. Add remaining onions and peas. Stir in thickener. When thickened, dish out.
- Stir in spring onion and coriander.

Note:
Store unused dough in a sealed plastic bag and refrigerate or freeze. Frozen pastry will keep for 1 month. To use, thaw out before rolling.

Preparation time: 60 minutes; Cooking time: 30 minutes; Baking time: 30 minutes
Oven setting: 175°C, 350°F, Gas Regulo 6; Makes : 22

LATTICE PINEAPPLE TARTS

INGREDIENTS

Plain (all-purpose) flour	150 g
Self-raising flour	180 g
Salt	1 pinch
Butter	165 g, cold and cut into small pieces
Egg	1, beaten
Water	less than 55 ml, cold
Pineapple jam*	1 recipe
Egg yolk	1, beaten
Evaporated milk	2 tsp

METHOD

- Sift flours into a mixing bowl. Add salt. Either rub in butter with fingers or blend with pastry cutter until mixture resembles breadcrumbs. Add beaten egg. Bind dough with water.
- On a lightly floured board, roll half the dough to 0.5-cm thickness. Cut 5-cm rounds with a plain cutter. Place rounds on squares of greaseproof paper. Repeat with other half of dough.
- Put 1 tsp pineapple jam on the centre of each round. Lay thin strips of dough over each lump of jam to form a lattice.
- Cut a ring of dough with a ring cutter. Fit ring around jam and over lattice. Use pastry pincers to pinch the edges of each tart for decoration.
- Place on cookie trays. Bake for 25–30 minutes. In the meantime, make glaze by beating egg yolk and milk together.
- If preferred, brush with glaze while still hot. Transfer to a wire rack to cool. Store in airtight containers.

*Pineapple Jam

INGREDIENTS:

Peeled pineapple	1 kg, finely blended (processed) and strained
Sugar	340 g
Screwpine (*pandan*) leaves	2–3
Vanilla essence (extract)	1 tsp

METHOD:

- Combine pineapple, sugar and screwpine leaves in a saucepan. Cook over low heat, stirring constantly until jam is dry. Add vanilla essence. Leave to cool. Use as required.

Preparation time: 30 minutes; Baking time: 30 minutes
Oven setting: 175°C, 350°F, Gas Regulo 6; Makes: 30

COCONUT TARTS

INGREDIENTS

Butter	250 g, cold and cut into small cubes ½ cup
Castor (superfine) sugar	60 g ¼ cup (2 round T.)
Egg yolk	1
Salt	1 pinch
Vanilla essence (extract)	1 tsp
Plain (all-purpose) flour	270 g, sifted 2 ¼ cup
Coconut filling*	1 recipe

METHOD

- Cream butter and sugar. Beat in egg yolk. Add salt and vanilla essence. Fold in sifted flour. Put mixture into a cookie press fitted with a star nozzle.
- Grease patty (shallow muffin) tins. Starting from the centre of each dip, pipe in circles until base is covered. Fill each cavity with coconut filling.
- Bake for 25–30 minutes until golden brown. Transfer to a wire rack to cool. Store in airtight containers.

*Coconut Filling

INGREDIENTS:

Egg	1
Castor (superfine) sugar	90 g 3 round T
Desiccated coconut	90 g

METHOD:

- Whisk egg and sugar. Stir in coconut.

Preparation time: 30 minutes; Cooking time: 10 minutes; Baking time: 25 minutes
Oven setting: 190°C, 375°F, Gas Regulo 7; Makes: 25

SARDINE ROLLS

INGREDIENTS

Pastry margarine	180 g, at room temperature
Kalamansi lime juice	from 2 limes
Water	175 ml, cold
Salt	1/4 tsp
Plain (all-purpose) flour	480 g
Baking powder	1 1/2 tsp
Butter	90 g, cold and diced
Egg	1, beaten
Filling*	1 recipe
Egg yolk	1, beaten
Evaporated milk	2 tsp

METHOD

- Between large, clean plastic sheets, roll pastry margarine into a 20 x 15-cm rectangle. Refrigerate.
- Combine lime juice, water and salt. Set aside.
- Sift flour and baking powder into a mixing bowl. Add cold butter and blend with pastry cutter or knife until mixture resembles breadcrumbs. Bind with egg and lime-juice mixture using a wooden spoon.
- On a lightly floured board, knead bowl's contents. Resulting dough should be soft but not sticky. Roll dough into a rectangle that has the width of margarine rectangle but twice the length; or 40 x 15 cm.
- Remove plastic sheets from margarine. Place in centre of dough rectangle. Fold over ends of dough to cover margarine. Seal edge.
- Roll dough parcel into a rectangle twice as long as it is wide. Fold rectangle into thirds widthways (widthwise). Repeat process of rolling and folding twice. Halve dough. Reserve one portion for future use.
- On a lightly floured board, roll other half to 2.5-mm thickness. Cut 10 x 6-cm pieces. Put 1 tsp sardine filling on one short end. Roll toward the other end. Seal edge with water.
- Place on ungreased cookie trays. Bake for 20–25 minutes or until golden brown. In the meantime, make glaze by beating egg yolk and milk together.
- When done, remove from oven and immediately brush with glaze.

*Sardine Filling

INGREDIENTS:

Cooking oil	1 Tbsp
Onion	1, peeled and finely chopped
Sardines	150g, mashed
Red chillies	2, seeded and finely sliced
Green chillies	2, seeded and finely sliced
Pepper	1 dash
Kalamansi lime juice	from 4 limes

METHOD:

- Heat oil in a wok. Fry chopped onion until fragrant. Add remaining ingredients. Fry until quite dry.

Preparation time: 60 minutes; Baking time: 20 minutes
Oven setting: 190°C, 375°F, Gas Regulo 7; Makes: 30

SAVOURY BOATS

INGREDIENTS

Plain (all-purpose) flour	240 g
Baking powder	1 tsp
Pastry margarine	120 g, at room temperature
Butter	45 g, softened at room temperature
Water	180–250 ml, cold
Egg yolk	1/2, beaten
Evaporated milk	1 tsp
Filling*	1 recipe

METHOD

- Sift flour and baking powder into a bowl. Thinly slice pastry margarine into flour with a knife. Either rub in with fingers or blend with pastry cutter until mixture resembles fine breadcrumbs.
- Mix in butter with cold water. Bind well. Resulting dough should be soft but not too sticky. Cover dough with dry cloth. Set aside for 15–30 minutes.
- On a floured board, roll dough to 1-cm thickness. Fold into thirds. Repeat process of rolling and folding twice. Halve dough for easier handling.
- Roll dough to 2.5-mm thickness. Cut pieces to line plain patty tins, or boat-shaped moulds. Trim excess off the edges.
- Bake for 20 minutes or until golden brown. In the meantime, make glaze by beating egg yolk and milk together.
- When done, remove from oven and immediately brush with glaze.
- Remove pastry shells from tins. Transfer to a wire rack to cool. Spoon filling onto cavity. Top with tomato strips just before serving.

*Filling

INGREDIENTS:

Chicken drumstick	1
Prawns (shrimps)	120 g, deveined
Cucumber	1, peeled, cored and diced
Coleslaw dressing	3 Tbsp
Pepper	1 dash
Salt	1 pinch
Tomato	1, ripe

METHOD:

- Season drumstick with salt, pepper and a little oil. Season prawns with salt and pepper. Steam both. When cooked, set aside to cool.
- Cut cooled chicken and prawns into small cubes. Combine meats and cucumber in a bowl. Stir in coleslaw dressing. Add pepper and salt to taste.
- Soak tomato in boiling water until its skin loosens or splits. Transfer to a bowl of cold water. Peel off skin. Halve peeled tomato. Squeeze out seeds. Cut remaining flesh into strips for garnish.

Note:
Unfilled shells keep well for up to 2 weeks in airtight containers.

Preparation time: 30 minutes; Baking time: 20 minutes
Oven setting: 190°C, 375°F, Gas Regulo 7; Makes: 30

SAVOURY PUFFS

INGREDIENTS

Plain (all-purpose) flour	150 g
Salt	1 pinch
Butter	120 g
Milk	180 ml, mixed with 55 ml water
Eggs	3, lightly beaten
Filling*	1 recipe

METHOD

- Line cookie trays with greased greaseproof paper.
- Sift flour into a mixing bowl. Add salt.
- Combine butter and milk in a small saucepan. Bring to the boil. Immediately pour into flour. Beat until paste becomes a soft ball. Leave to cool slightly.
- Beat in eggs one spoonful at a time. Dough should hold its shape when piped but must not be too stiff.
- Fit a pipe with a 1-cm wide nozzle. Pipe small rounds or 5-cm lengths onto lined cookie trays, well apart to allow spreading.
- Bake for 15–20 minutes or until puffed up and pale golden. Transfer to a wire rack to cool.
- Just before serving, make slits along bases of puffs. Fill with savoury filling.

*Filling

INGREDIENTS:

Cooked chicken	240 g, diced
Cucumber	1/2, peeled, cored and diced
Tomatoes	2, peeled and seeded (see p. 112)
Salt and pepper	to taste
Coleslaw dressing	3 Tbsp

METHOD:

- Combine all ingredients, except coleslaw dressing. Mix well. Add dressing.

Preparation time: 90 minutes; Baking time: 20 minutes
Oven setting: 190°C, 375°F, Gas Regulo 7; Makes: 40

SAVOURY HORNS

INGREDIENTS

Plain (all-purpose) flour	480 g
Baking powder	2 tsp
Pastry margarine	240 g, at room temperature
Butter	75–90 g, softened at room temperature
Water	360–500 ml, cold
Egg yolk	1, beaten
Evaporated milk	2 tsp
Savoury filling*	1 recipe
Sweet cream**	1 recipe

METHOD

- Sift flour and baking powder into a bowl. Thinly slice pastry margarine into flour with a knife. Either rub in with fingers or blend with pastry cutter until mixture resembles fine breadcrumbs.
- Mix in butter with cold water. Bind well. Resulting dough should be soft but not too sticky. Cover dough with dry cloth. Set aside for 15–30 minutes.
- On a floured board, roll dough to 1-cm thickness. Fold into thirds. Repeat process of rolling and folding twice. Halve dough for easier handling.
- Roll dough to 2.5-mm thickness. Cut 30 x 1-cm pieces.
- Wind each piece around a cream horn tin, from point to wide end, overlapping slightly all the time.
- Place on ungreased trays, with exposed end of final round against tray's surface.
- Bake for 20 minutes or until golden. In the meantime, make glaze by beating egg yolk and milk together. When done, remove from oven and immediately brush with glaze.
- When cold, fill with savoury filling or sweet cream. Serve immediately.

*Filling

INGREDIENTS:

Cucumber	1, large, peeled, cored and diced
Tomato	1, ripe, blanched, peeled and seeded
Crabmeat or chopped chicken	240 g, cooked
Thousand Island dressing	2–3 Tbsp
Pepper	1 dash
Salt	1 pinch

METHOD:

- Put crabmeat, cucumber and tomato into a bowl. Stir in salad dressing. Add pepper and salt to taste.

**Sweet Cream

INGREDIENTS:

Butter	250 g, cold and cut into small cubes
Icing (confectioners') sugar	150 g, sifted
Vanilla essence (extract)	1 tsp
Evaporated milk	1 small can (170 g), chilled
Brandy	2 Tbsp

METHOD:

- Cream butter pieces and sugar until light and creamy. Add essence. Beat in evaporated milk a little at a time, then brandy.

Note: Unfilled and unglazed horns keep well in airtight containers for up to 2 weeks.

breads

Preparation time: 15 minutes; Cooking time: 15 minutes
Makes: 10

VANILLA DOUGHNUTS

INGREDIENTS

Milk	105 ml
Water	85 ml
Corn oil	1/2 Tbsp
Plain (all-purpose) flour	180 g
Baking powder	1 tsp
Sugar	1 Tbsp
Salt	1 pinch
Egg	1, lightly beaten
Cooking oil for deep-frying	
Castor (superfine) sugar	

METHOD

- Mix milk, water and corn oil together. Set aside.
- Sift flour and baking powder into a bowl. Stir in sugar and salt.
- Pour milk mixture into sifted ingredients. Mix with a spoon. Stir in beaten egg. Do not beat mixture.
- Spoon batter into doughnut maker. Lower doughnuts into hot oil. When they float, turn immediately. Fry both sides until brown.
- Coat with castor sugar.

Preparation time: 30 minutes; Baking time: 15 minutes
Oven Setting: 205°C, 400°F, Gas Regulo 8; Makes: 14

CHEESE-AND-BACON SCONES

INGREDIENTS

Egg yolk	1, beaten
Water	1 tsp
Self-raising flour	240 g
Margarine	60 g
Cheddar cheese	90 g, grated
Bacon	90 g, chopped
Milk	170 ml

METHOD

- Beat egg yolk and water together to make glaze. Set aside.
- Sift flour into a bowl. Lightly rub in margarine with fingers or blend with a pastry cutter. Stir in cheese and bacon. Mix with milk to form soft dough.
- On a lightly floured board, roll dough to 1–2-cm thickness. Cut 5–6 cm rounds. Place on lightly greased trays. Brush with glaze.
- Bake for 12–15 minutes or until golden brown.
- Scones can be served halved lengthways (lengthwise) to sandwich tomato slices.

Preparation time: 120 minutes; Baking time: 25 minutes
Oven Setting: 205°C, 400°F, Gas Regulo 8; Makes: 15

BACON PARSLEY ROLLS

INGREDIENTS

Sugar	1 Tbsp
Water	225 ml, lukewarm
Fresh yeast	2.5-cm cube
Plain (all-purpose) flour	360 g, sifted
Corn oil	$^1/_2$ Tbsp
Egg white (A)	1, lightly beaten
Bacon	120 g, cut into tiny squares
Coriander (cilantro) leaves	1 sprig, chopped
Egg white (B)	$^1/_2$, beaten
Water	1 Tbsp

METHOD

- Dissolve sugar in lukewarm water. Drop in yeast. Let stand for about 15 minutes until frothy.
- Sift half the flour into a mixing bowl. Add corn oil, egg white (A) and yeast liquid. Beat mixture thoroughly. Stir in remaining flour.
- On a floured board, knead dough until smooth and no longer sticks to hands.
- Return dough to bowl. Cover with damp cloth. Leave for about 60 minutes until dough doubles in volume. Punch dough down and let rise again.
- On a floured board, knead dough. Add bacon and coriander. Knead until ingredients are well combined. Keep board and hands amply floured to prevent dough from sticking.
- Shape dough into a long roll. Cut 15–17 similarly sized pieces. Roll each piece into a rectangular shape. Place well apart on greased baking trays.
- Just before baking, place a pan half-filled with boiling water on oven's bottom shelf.
- Bake for 25–30 minutes or until golden brown. In the meantime, make glaze by beating egg white (B) and 1 Tbsp water together.
- About 5 minutes before removing from oven, brush with glaze. Transfer to a wire rack to cool.

Preparation time: 120 minutes; Cooking time: 15 minutes; Baking time: 15 minutes
Oven Setting: 205°C, 400°F, Gas Regulo 8; Makes: 24

COCONUT BUNS

INGREDIENTS

Sugar	1 Tbsp
Water	115 ml, lukewarm
Fresh yeast	2.5-cm cube
Plain (all-purpose) flour	360 g
Salt	1/2 tsp
Butter	60 g, softened at room temperature
Milk	85 ml
Filling*	1 recipe
Egg yolk	1, beaten
Evaporated milk	1 tsp

METHOD

- Dissolve sugar in water. Drop in yeast. Let stand for about 15 minutes until frothy.
- Sift flour into a bowl. Add salt. Mix in butter with a knife or blend with a pastry cutter until mixture resembles breadcrumbs. Pour in milk and yeast liquid. Mix with a wooden spoon. Work with hands to form firm dough.
- On a floured board, knead dough until smooth. Return dough to bowl. Cover with a damp cloth. Leave for about 60 minutes until dough doubles in volume. Punch dough down and let rise again.
- On a floured board, knead and form a long roll. Cut 24 similarly sized pieces. Shape pieces into balls. Flatten balls and roll into rounds.
- Put a teaspoonful of filling on the centre of each round. Fold in edges and seal. Reshape parcels into balls. Place well apart on greased trays. Leave to rise for about 10 minutes.
- Bake for 15–20 minutes. In the meantime, make glaze by beating egg yolk and milk together.
- Remove from oven and immediately brush with glaze. Transfer to a wire rack to cool.

*Filling

INGREDIENTS

Corn oil	115 ml
Palm sugar (*gula Melaka*)	180 g, cut into small pieces
Skinned coconut	1, grated
Salt	1 pinch

METHOD

- Heat oil in a wok. Melt palm sugar over medium heat. Add coconut and salt. Fry until evenly coated with palm syrup. Dish out. Leave to cool.

Preparation time: 120 minutes; Baking time: 25 minutes
Oven Setting: 175°C, 350°F, Gas Regulo 6; Makes: 14

GRANDMA'S PINWHEELS

INGREDIENTS

Sugar	1 Tbsp
Milk	225 ml, warm
Fresh yeast	2.5 x 5-cm piece
Plain (all-purpose) flour	480 g, sifted
Salt	1 pinch
Lard or corn oil	1 cup
Eggs	4, beaten
Jam	quantity and flavour as desired
Chopped nuts (optional)	130 g
Coarse white sugar	

METHOD

- Dissolve sugar in milk. Drop in yeast. Let stand for about 15 minutes until frothy.
- Sift flour into a bowl. Add salt and lard or corn oil. Mix by hand until ingredients well combined. Add beaten eggs. Mix well. Stir in yeast liquid. Beat until smooth. Leave for about 90 minutes until dough doubles in volume.
- On a floured board, roll half the dough into a 30 x 35-cm rectangle. Spread on jam. Sprinkle nuts, if used, over the top. Roll up Swiss-roll style. With a flour-coated knife, cut 2-cm wide pieces. Repeat with remaining dough.
- Carefully place on greased baking trays. Sprinkle coarse sugar over the top. Bake for 25–30 minutes.

Preparation time: 150 minutes; Cooking time: 15 minutes; Baking time: 15 minutes
Oven Setting: 205°C, 400°F, Gas Regulo 8; Makes: 24

CURRY BUNS

INGREDIENTS

Water	225 ml, warm
Milk	225 ml
Sugar	2 Tbsp
Fresh yeast	30 g
Plain (all-purpose) flour	720 g
Salt	1 1/2 tsp
Butter	90 g, softened at room temperature
Filling*	1 recipe
Egg yolk	1, beaten
Evaporated milk	2 tsp

METHOD

- Mix half the warm water and milk. Set aside.
- Dissolve sugar in remaining warm water. Drop in yeast. Let stand for about 15 minutes until frothy.
- Sift flour into a mixing bowl. Add salt. Stir butter into flour. Add diluted milk and yeast liquid. Bind with a wooden spoon.
- On a lightly floured board, knead dough until crack-free. Return dough to bowl. Cover with damp cloth. Leave for about 90 minutes until dough doubles in volume. Punch dough down and let rise again.
- On a floured board, knead dough and form a long roll. Cut 24 similarly sized pieces. Shape pieces into small balls. Flatten balls and roll into rounds.
- Put a teaspoonful of filling on the centre of each round. Fold in edges and seal. Reshape parcels into smooth balls. Place well apart on greased trays. Leave to rise for 10–15 minutes
- Bake for 15–20 minutes until golden brown. In the meantime, make glaze by beating egg yolk and evaporated milk together.
- Remove from oven and immediately brush with glaze.

Filling*

INGREDIENTS

Chicken, beef or pork	240 g, cut into small cubes
Curry powder (p. 109)	2 Tbsp
Cooking oil	2 Tbsp
Onions	2, diced or blended (processed)
Potatoes	2, medium, cut into small cubes
Salt	1 tsp
Monosodium glutamate (optional)	1/2 tsp

METHOD

- Season meat with curry powder. Set aside.
- Heat oil in a wok. Lightly brown onions. Add potatoes. Fry until soft with a little water.
- Add seasoned meat. Stir-fry until cooked. Add salt and monosodium glutamate if used.
- Fry filling until dry. Dish out. Leave to cool.

Note: Unfilled and unglazed horns keep well in airtight containers for up to 2 weeks.

Preparation time: 120 minutes; Baking time: 30 minutes
Oven Setting: 205°C, 400°F, Gas Regulo 8

CRUSTY ROLL

INGREDIENTS

Sugar	1 Tbsp
Water	225 ml, lukewarm
Fresh yeast	2.5-cm cube
Plain (all-purpose) flour	360 g, sifted
Corn oil	1/2 Tbsp
Salt	1 tsp
Egg white (A)	1, lightly beaten
Egg white (B)	1/2, beaten
Water	1 Tbsp

METHOD

- Dissolve sugar in lukewarm water. Drop in yeast. Let stand for about 15 minutes until frothy.
- Sift half the flour into a mixing bowl. Add corn oil, salt, egg white (A) and yeast liquid. Beat mixture thoroughly. Stir in remaining flour.
- On a floured board, knead dough until smooth and no longer sticks to hands. Return dough to bowl. Cover with a damp cloth. Leave for about 60 minutes until dough doubles in volume. Punch dough down and let rise again.
- On a floured board, knead then divide dough into three equal portions. Shape each portion into a 30-cm long roll.
- Plait (braid) three rolls together. Secure at both ends. Place on greased baking tray. Brush with water. Let rise until double in volume.
- Just before baking, place a pan half-filled with boiling water on oven's bottom shelf.
- Bake for 15 minutes. Lower temperature to 175°C, 350°F or Gas Regulo 6. Bake for 12 minutes more or until golden brown. In the meantime, make glaze by beating egg white (B) and 1 Tbsp water together.
- About 5 minutes before removing from oven, brush with glaze or more water.

Note: For French bread, divide dough into two portions instead of three. Form each portion into a long roll. Brush with water, then cut diagonal slits across the top with a sharp knife.

Preparation time: 120 minutes; Cooking time: 15 minutes; Baking time: 20 minutes
Oven Setting: 205°C, 400°F, Gas Regulo 8

PIZZA

INGREDIENTS

Sugar	1/2 Tbsp
Water	115 ml, lukewarm
Fresh yeast	15 g
Plain (all-purpose) flour	240 g
Salt	1 pinch
Corn oil	2 tsp
Tomato sauce*	1 recipe
Grated cheese	

METHOD

- Dissolve sugar in water. Drop in yeast. Let stand for 15 minutes until liquid frothy.
- Sift flour into a mixing bowl. Add salt and corn oil. Blend with a pastry cutter. Add yeast liquid. Mix with a wooden spoon.
- On a lightly floured board, knead dough until smooth. Return dough to bowl. Cover with damp cloth. Leave until dough doubles in volume. Punch dough down and let rise again.
- On a floured board, roll dough to fit well-greased 17.5 x 27.5-cm baking tray. Leave to rise for 10–15 minutes.
- Spread on tomato sauce. Bake for 20–25 minutes. Sprinkle cheese over the top either before or after baking.

*Tomato Sauce

INGREDIENTS:

Tomatoes	360 g, ripe
Beef or pork	180 g, minced
Sugar	1/2 tsp
Pepper	1 dash
Salt	1/2 tsp
Cooking oil	1 Tbsp
Garlic	3 cloves, minced
Shallots	3, sliced
Tomato purée	4 tsp

METHOD

- Soak tomatoes in boiling water for 5 minutes or until skins become loose or split. Transfer to a bowl of cold water. Peel off skins. Roughly chop peeled tomatoes. Set aside.
- Season meat with sugar, pepper and salt.
- Heat oil in a wok. Lightly brown garlic and shallots. Add seasoned meat. Stir-fry for a few minutes. Dish out.
- Put tomatoes into wok. Simmer gently until quite dry. Add tomato purée and meat. Adjust to taste with more pepper, salt and sugar. Dish out. Leave to cool.

savouries

Preparation time: 90 minutes; Cooking time: 12 minutes
Makes: 40

SIEW MAI

Siew mai are steamed meat dumplings and are a popular type of *dim sum*.

INGREDIENTS

Wantan (dumpling) skins	150 g, 7.5-cm square pieces
Filling*	1 recipe
Cooked crab roe	1 Tbsp

METHOD

- Cut *wantan* skins into 7.5-cm rounds with cutter. Put 2 tsp filling on each centre. Gather edges of skin and smooth toward the top, pleating will occur naturally.
- Place in greased bamboo baskets. Decorate with crab roe on top. Steam for 12 minutes.

*Filling

INGREDIENTS:

Peeled prawns (shrimps)	240 g, deveined and well minced
Fatty pork	240 g, minced
Crabmeat	120 g, cooked
Salt	1 tsp
Sesame seed oil	1/2 tsp
Monosodium glutamate (optional)	1 dash
Pepper	1 dash
Egg white	1
Corn flour (cornstarch)	1 1/2 Tbsp
Corn oil	1 Tbsp
Dried Chinese mushrooms	2, soaked, stems discarded and minced
Water chestnuts	3, peeled and minced
Spring onion (scallion)	1 stalk, thinly sliced

METHOD:

- Combine prawns, pork and crabmeat. Season with salt, sesame seed oil, monosodium glutamate, pepper and egg white. Stir in corn flour and corn oil. Beat mixture with a spoon.
- Mix in mushrooms, water chestnuts and spring onion. Refrigerate for 60 minutes.

Note: If crab roe is unavailable, set aside 1 Tbsp filling, stir in 2 drops orange food colouring and use as decorative topping.

Preparation time: 150 minutes; Cooking time: 30 minutes
Makes: 32

CHAR SIEW POW

INGREDIENTS

Sugar	115 g
Water	340 ml, lukewarm
Fresh yeast	30 g
Plain (all-purpose) flour	675 g
Baking powder	1/2 Tbsp
Bicarbonate of (baking) soda	1/3 tsp
Salt	1 tsp
Corn oil	1 Tbsp
Char siew (grilled pork) filling*	1 recipe

METHOD

- Dissolve sugar in water. Drop in yeast. Let stand for 10–15 minutes until frothy.
- Sift powdered ingredients into a bowl. Add salt. Gradually pour in corn oil and yeast liquid, stirring with a wooden spoon. When mixture becomes too difficult for the spoon, use hands to form firm dough.
- On a lightly floured board, knead dough for at least 10 minutes. Sprinkle flour occasionally to prevent dough from sticking to the board.
- Return dough to bowl. Cover with a damp cloth. Leave for about 90 minutes until dough doubles in volume. Punch dough down and let rise again for 20–30 minutes.
- On a lightly floured board, knead dough until smooth. Form two rolls, each 4 cm in diameter. Cut 2-cm wide pieces.
- Flatten each piece with a roller. Put a teaspoonful of filling on the centre. To gather edges, lift one side and form pleats in one direction. Twist pleats together at the very top to secure.
- Place buns (*pow*) on rounds of greaseproof paper. Arrange well apart in bamboo baskets.
- Bring water in steamer to the boil over high heat. Steam for 12 minutes.

*Char Siew Filling

INGREDIENTS:

Streaky pork or skinless chicken	600 g
Salt	2 tsp
Sugar	3 Tbsp
Light soy sauce	1 Tbsp
Dark soy sauce	1/2 tsp
Red food colouring	a few drops
Water	450 ml
Oyster sauce	2 tsp
Sesame seed oil	1/2 tsp
Corn flour (cornstarch)	2 tsp
Coriander (cilantro) leaves	1 sprig, chopped

METHOD:

- Wash pork, then dry with a tea towel. Cut 2.5-cm strips. Season with salt, sugar, and soy sauces. Add food colouring. Marinate for at least 120 minutes or overnight in the refrigerator.
- Place pork pieces on wire mesh. Oven grill with a pan of water on the bottom shelf. Turn pieces occasionally until cooked. Remove pork from mesh and reserve gravy. Dice cooled pork.
- Combine 4 Tbsp gravy, oyster sauce, sesame seed oil and corn flour in a wok. Bring to the boil. Stir in diced pork and coriander. Dish out. Leave to cool.

SPICY CHICKPEAS

INGREDIENTS

Chickpeas (*kacang kuda putih* or *channa dhal*)	600 g, soaked overnight in water
Salt	1 tsp
Cooking oil	2 Tbsp
Onions	3, large, peeled and minced
Garlic	1 clove, peeled and minced
Ginger	4-cm piece, peeled and minced
Ground saffron	$^1/_2$ tsp
Ground chilli	1 Tbsp
Cumin	2 tsp, toasted and ground
Tamarind pulp (*asam Jawa*)	1 Tbsp, mixed with a little water and strained
Salt	to taste

METHOD

- Cook chickpeas in pressure cooker for 10 minutes with enough water to cover and salt. Remove from cooker. Briefly mash with a spoon so contents are still coarse.
- Heat oil in a wok. Lightly brown onions, garlic and ginger. Add chickpeas, saffron, chilli and cumin. Stir in tamarind liquid. Bring to the boil and sustain a while. Add salt to taste.

Preparation time: 15 minutes; Cooking time: 75 minutes
Serves 8–10

NASI KUNYIT

Nasi means "rice" in Malay and *kunyit* "turmeric". Altogether, then, *nasi kunyit* refers to turmeric-flavoured rice, a long-time classic and favourite in Malay cuisine.

INGREDIENTS

Dried turmeric (*kunyit*)	4 large pieces
Glutinous rice	1.25 kg, washed and drained
Salt	$1^1/_2$ tsp
Banana leaves	
Coconut milk	500 ml, squeezed from $2^1/_2$ grated coconuts and sufficient water

METHOD

- Crush turmeric and wrap with a clean cloth. Soak rice overnight in enough water to cover with turmeric and 1 tsp salt added.
- Line base of shallow bamboo basket with banana leaves. Transfer rice to basket. Steam for 60 minutes or until rice is cooked and soft.
- Transfer rice to heatproof (flameproof) dish or pot. Stir in coconut milk and remaining salt. Return rice to steamer for 10–15 minutes.
- Dish out onto plate. Shape into mound by lightly pressing with spoon. Serve with Chicken Curry (p. 158).

Preparation time: 150 minutes; Cooking time: 12 minutes
Makes: 14

STEAMED FLOWER BUNS

INGREDIENTS

Sugar	2 Tbsp
Water	3 Tbsp, lukewarm
Fresh yeast	21 g
Plain (all-purpose) flour	450 g
Baking powder	1 tsp
Bicarbonate of (baking) soda	1/3 tsp
Salt	1 tsp
Milk	180 ml, mixed with 55 ml water
Corn oil	

METHOD

- Dissolve sugar in water. Drop in yeast. Let stand for 10–15 minutes until frothy.
- Sift powdered ingredients into a bowl. Add salt. Gradually pour in milk and yeast liquid, stirring with a wooden spoon. When dough becomes too difficult for the spoon, use hands to form firm dough.
- On a floured board, knead dough for 10 minutes or until smooth. Return dough to bowl. Cover with a damp cloth. Leave for 90 minutes until dough doubles in volume. Punch dough down and let rise again for 20–30 minutes.
- On a floured board, knead for 5 minutes or until smooth. Halve dough. Roll each half into a 12.5 x 30-cm rectangle. Brush with corn oil. Carefully roll up lengthways (lengthwise) Swiss-roll style. Cut 2.5-cm wide pieces.
- Stack two pieces to form a standing figure 8, with swirls facing you. With a flour-coated chopstick, press down lengthways (lengthwise), or parallel to swirls, along centre of top edge. To secure the joining of two pieces, pinch them together at both ends of chopstick-marked line.
- Place buns on squares of greaseproof paper. Arrange well apart in bamboo baskets.
- Bring water in steamer to the boil over high heat. Steam for 12 minutes.

Preparation time: 30 minutes; Cooking time: 30 minutes
Makes: 12

SAVOURY PANCAKES

INGREDIENTS

Cooking oil	3 Tbsp
Shallots	3, peeled and sliced
Dried prawns (shrimps)	75 g, soaked and minced
Plain (all-purpose) flour	300 g
Water	450 ml
Salt	1/4 tsp
Pepper	1/4 tsp
Spring onions (scallions)	2–3 stalks, finely sliced

METHOD

- Heat oil in a nonstick pan. Fry shallots until light brown and crisp. Drain and set aside.
- Add dried prawns to wok. Fry over low heat until fragrant and crisp. Drain and set aside. Remove oil and reserve for frying pancakes later.
- Sift flour into a bowl. Stir in water to make smooth, runny batter. Strain batter if lumpy. Stir in salt, pepper and spring onions. Mix in crispy shallots and prawns.
- Lightly grease nonstick pan. Pour in ladleful of batter. Fry both sides until lightly brown.
- When cool, roll up Swiss-roll style. Serve with chilli sauce.

Preparation time: 30 minutes; Cooking time: 30 minutes
Makes: 24

PURIS

Puri is a type of bread in South Asian cuisine and is readily identified by its inflated appearance.

INGREDIENTS

Wholemeal (*atta*) flour	240 g
Plain (all-purpose) flour	120 g
Semolina	60 g
Salt	1 tsp
Corn oil	4 tsp
Cooking oil for deep-frying	

METHOD

- Sift flours and semolina into a bowl. Add salt and corn oil. Knead into firm dough with a little water.
- Shape dough into small balls. On a floured board, flatten balls into thin rounds with a roller.
- Deep-fry in hot oil until *puri* is inflated and light brown. Serve hot with Spicy Chickpeas (p. 138) or curries.

Preparation time: 150 minutes; Cooking time: 75 minutes
Makes: 32

TAU SAR POW

INGREDIENTS

Sugar	115 g
Water	340 ml, lukewarm
Fresh yeast	30 g
Plain (all-purpose) flour	675 g
Baking powder	$^1/_2$ Tbsp
Bicarbonate of (baking) soda	$^1/_3$ tsp
Salt	1 tsp
Corn oil	1 Tbsp
Tau sar (red bean paste) filling*	1 recipe

METHOD

- Dissolve sugar in water. Drop in yeast. Let stand for 10–15 minutes until frothy.
- Sift powdered ingredients into a bowl. Add salt. Gradually pour in corn oil and yeast liquid, stirring with a wooden spoon. When mixture becomes too difficult for the spoon, use hands to form firm dough.
- On a lightly floured board, knead dough for at least 10 minutes. Sprinkle flour occasionally to prevent dough sticking to the board.
- Return dough to bowl. Cover with a damp cloth. Leave for 90 minutes until dough doubles in volume. Punch dough down and let rise again for 20–30 minutes.
- On a lightly floured board, knead dough until smooth. Form two rolls, each 4 cm in diameter. Cut 2-cm wide pieces.
- Flatten each piece with a roller. Put a ball of filling on the centre. To gather edges, lift one side and form pleats in one direction. Twist pleats together at the very top to secure.
- Place buns (*pow*) on rounds of greaseproof paper. Arrange well apart in bamboo baskets.
- Bring water in steamer to the boil over high heat. Steam for 12 minutes.

****Tau Sar* Filling**

INGREDIENTS:

Red beans	450 g
Screwpine (*pandan*) leaves	3–4
Water	2.25 l
Cooking oil	280 ml
Sugar	600 g
Vanilla essence (extract)	1 tsp

METHOD:

- Wash red beans and screwpine leaves. Put both into a pressure cooker. Add water. Cook for 40 minutes until beans are soft.
- Blend (process) pressure cooker's contents into a fine paste. If beans are too dry and not turning in the blender, add a little hot water.
- Heat oil in a wok. Add bean paste and sugar. Stirring all the time, cook bean paste until quite dry. Add vanilla essence. Transfer to a bowl. Leave to cool.
- When bowl's contents are at room temperature, refrigerate. When chilled, shape teaspoonfuls of paste into small balls by rolling between palms.

Preparation time: 150 minutes; Cooking time: 15 minutes
Makes: 32

TURNIP-AND-CHICKEN POW

INGREDIENTS

Sugar	115 g
Water	340 ml, lukewarm
Fresh yeast	30 g
Plain (all-purpose) flour	675 g
Baking powder	1/2 Tbsp
Bicarbonate of (baking) soda	1/3 tsp
Salt	1 tsp
Corn oil	1 Tbsp
Filling*	1 recipe

METHOD

- Dissolve sugar in water. Drop in yeast. Let stand for 10–15 minutes until frothy.
- Sift powdered ingredients into a bowl. Add salt. Gradually pour in corn oil and yeast liquid, stirring with a wooden spoon. When mixture becomes too difficult for the spoon, use hands to form firm dough.
- On a lightly floured board, knead dough for at least 10 minutes. Sprinkle flour occasionally to prevent dough sticking to the board.
- Return dough to bowl. Cover with a damp cloth. Leave for 90 minutes until dough doubles in volume. Punch dough down and let rise again for 20–30 minutes.
- On a lightly floured board, knead dough until smooth. Form two rolls, each 4 cm in diameter. Cut 2-cm wide pieces.
- Flatten each piece with a roller. Put a teaspoonful of filling on the centre. To gather edges, lift one side and form pleats in one direction. Twist pleats together at the very top to secure.
- Place buns (*pow*) on rounds of greaseproof paper. Arrange well apart in bamboo baskets.
- Bring water in steamer to the boil over high heat. Steam for 12 minutes.

*Filling

INGREDIENTS:

Chicken or pork	300 g, diced
Light soy sauce	1 tsp
Dark soy sauce	1/2 Tbsp
Sesame seed oil	1 tsp
Salt	1 tsp
Pepper	1 dash
Monosodium glutamate (optional)	1/4 tsp
Cooking oil	4 Tbsp
Turnip	450 g, peeled and diced
Onions	2, large, peeled and diced
Corn flour (cornstarch)	3 tsp, mixed with a little water to make thickener
Coriander (cilantro) leaves	2 sprigs, chopped

METHOD:

- Season meat with soy sauces, sesame seed oil, salt, pepper and monosodium glutamate.
- Heat sufficient oil in wok to fry turnip. When done, dish out and set aside.
- Heat remaining oil in wok. Lightly brown onions. Add chicken and stir-fry. Add cooked turnip. Add thickener a bit at a time. Stir in coriander. Dish out. Leave to cool.

Preparation time: 45 minutes; Cooking time: 15 minutes
Makes: 60

FRIED WANTAN

Wantan means "dumplings" in Cantonese. *Wantan* can be served boiled in soup or fried.

INGREDIENTS

Wantan (dumpling) skins	150 g, 7.5-cm square pieces
Egg white	1, beaten
Filling*	1 recipe
Cooking oil for deep-frying	

METHOD

- Turn square *wantan* skin 45 degrees so that square becomes diamond looking on.
- Put a few prawn pieces near bottom corner of diamond. Fold lowest tip over prawns to meet centre of diamond.
- From folded edge, roll up until just past widest part of diamond.
- Lift both ends of rolled section, position above filling, then stick together using beaten egg white.
- Heat oil in a wok. Deep-fry until golden. Serve hot with chilli sauce.

*Filling

INGREDIENTS:

Prawns (shrimps)	120 g, small–medium
Egg white	$^1/_2$
Light soy sauce	1 tsp
Sugar	$^1/_2$ tsp
Salt	1 pinch
Pepper	1 dash
Monosodium glutamate (optional)	1 dash
Spring onion (scallion)	1 stalk, finely sliced
Coriander (cilantro) leaves	1 sprig, chopped

METHOD:

- Peel and wash prawns. Dry with a tea towel. Cut each prawn into 2–3 pieces.
- Season with egg white, light soy sauce, sugar, salt, pepper and monosodium glutamate for at least 30 minutes.
- Mix in spring onion and coriander.

Preparation time: 60 minutes; Cooking time: 15 minutes
Makes: 50

PRAWN BALLS

INGREDIENTS

Prawns (shrimps)	600 g, small–medium
Light soy sauce	2 tsp
Sesame seed oil	1 tsp
Salt	1/2 tsp
Sugar	1/2 tsp
Pepper	1 dash
Monosodium glutamate (optional)	1 dash
Egg white	1/2
Corn flour (cornstarch)	1 tsp
Spring onions (scallions)	2 stalks, finely sliced
Coriander (cilantro) leaves	1 sprig, finely sliced
Water chestnuts	4, peeled and minced
Bread	1 1/2 loaves, 1-day old and cut into very small cubes
Cooking oil for deep-frying	

METHOD

- Peel and wash prawns. Dry with a tea towel. Mince to a fine paste.
- Season with soy sauce, sesame seed oil, salt, sugar, pepper, monosodium glutamate, egg white and corn flour. Stir in spring onions, coriander and water chestnuts. Refrigerate for at least 30 minutes.
- Drop teaspoonfuls of mixture onto bread cubes. Form bread-coated balls. Deep-fry over low heat until golden. Serve with chilli sauce.

Chilli Sauce

INGREDIENTS:

Red chillies	12, large and seeded
Garlic	3 cloves, peeled
Water	225 ml
Tomato sauce	2 Tbsp
Vinegar	1/2 Tbsp
Sugar	1/2 Tbsp
Salt	1/4 tsp
Cooking oil	1 Tbsp

METHOD:

- Blend (process) chillies, garlic and water into a fine paste. Transfer to a small saucepan.
- Add remaining ingredients. Bring to the boil. When cool, store in glass jars at room temperature.

Preparation time: 60 minutes; Cooking time: 30 minutes
Makes: 45

FRIED SPRING ROLLS

INGREDIENTS

Spring roll skins	1 packet (approximately 50 pieces), 12.5-cm square pieces
Egg white	1, beaten
Filling*	1 recipe
Cooking oil for deep-frying	

METHOD

- Position spring roll skin such that it is a square looking on.
- About 2 cm away from bottom edge, spread 1 Tbsp filling along length.
- Fold in left and right edges. Gently roll up. Seal with egg white.
- Deep-fry rolls in hot oil. Serve with chilli sauce.

*Filling

INGREDIENTS:

Chicken or pork	240 g, cut into thin strips
Peeled prawns (shrimps)	240 g, deveined and diced
Corn flour (cornstarch)	1 tsp
Salt	1/2 tsp
Sugar	1 1/2 tsp
Light soy sauce	3 tsp
Dark soy sauce	1 tsp
Five-spice powder	1/2 tsp
Pepper	1 dash
Cooking oil	3 Tbsp
Garlic	4 cloves, peeled and minced
Dried Chinese mushrooms	4, soaked, stems discarded and diced
Turnip	600 g, peeled, shredded and squeezed of excess water
Carrot	1, small, shredded
Corn flour (cornstarch)	2 tsp, mixed with a little water to make thickener
Spring onion (scallion)	1 stalk, chopped
Coriander (cilantro) leaves	1 sprig, chopped

METHOD:

- Season meat and prawns with corn flour, salt, 1/2 tsp sugar and 1 tsp light soy sauce. Set aside.
- To make seasoning, combine remaining sugar and light soy sauce, dark soy sauce, five-spice powder and pepper. Set aside.
- Heat oil in a wok. Lightly brown garlic. Add meat and prawns. Stir-fry, then dish out.
- Fry mushrooms for 1 minute. Add turnip and carrot. Fry well. Stir in meat and prawns. Add seasoning. Add thickener a bit at a time. Stir in spring onion and coriander. Dish out. Leave to cool.

Preparation time: 60 minutes; Cooking time: 15 minutes
Makes: 34

YAM PUFFS

INGREDIENTS

Yam	1.25 kg, peeled and cubed
Sugar	2 Tbsp
Salt	1 tsp
Monosodium glutamate (optional)	1 tsp
Tapioca flour	3 Tbsp
Five-spice powder	1 pinch
Corn oil	2 Tbsp
Filling*	1 recipe
Cooking oil for deep-frying	

METHOD

- Steam yam pieces for 25–30 minutes until soft. While hot, mash until lump-free. Add remaining ingredients. Knead well. Shape into golf ball-like pieces.
- With lightly floured hands, flatten balls into rounds. Put a teaspoonful of filling in each centre. Bring edges together over filling. Seal with a little water.
- Deep-fry until golden brown.

*Filling

INGREDIENTS:

Sugar	1 tsp
Salt	1/2 tsp
Light soy sauce	1 tsp
Oyster sauce	1 tsp
Monosodium glutamate (optional)	1/2 tsp
Water	4 Tbsp
Corn flour (cornstarch)	1/2 Tbsp
Cooking oil	2 Tbsp
Garlic	4 cloves, peeled and chopped
Dried Chinese mushrooms	2–3, soaked, stems discarded and diced
Peeled prawns (shrimps)	120 g, diced
Chicken	180 g, cut into small cubes
Green peas	30 g
Coriander (cilantro) leaves	1 sprig, chopped
Spring onion (scallion)	1 stalk, chopped

METHOD:

- Combine sugar, salt, light soy and oyster sauces, monosodium glutamate, water and corn flour. Set aside.
- Heat oil in a wok. Lightly brown garlic. Add mushrooms and stir-fry. Add prawns and chicken. Fry for 1 minute. Add peas and combined ingredients. Mix in coriander and spring onion. Dish out. Leave to cool.

Note:
Serve buns with chicken curry, chicken stew or pork stew.

Preparation time: 30 minutes; Cooking time: 30 minutes
Makes: 24

ROTI JALA

Roti jala is a type of thin bread in Malay cuisine and is readily identified by its doily-like appearance.

INGREDIENTS

Plain (all-purpose) flour	240 g
Salt	1/2 tsp
Eggs	2, beaten
Coconut milk	565 ml, squeezed from 1/2 grated, skinned coconut and sufficient water

METHOD

- Sift flour into a bowl. Add salt. Stir in eggs and coconut milk. Beat until smooth. Strain batter if lumpy.
- Grease a nonstick pan. Place over low heat. Position *roti jala* cup over pan. Put in a ladleful of batter. Move cup in a circular motion to make lacy pattern. Cook until shape sets. Transfer to a dish. Repeat until batter is used up.
- When cool, fold pancakes in eighths or fold and roll up. Serve with Curry Kapitan (p. 156).

Note: To make *roti jala*, a special cup, with four funnels extending from the base, is necessary.

Preparation time: 30 minutes; Cooking time: 40 minutes
Serves 8

CURRY KAPITAN

INGREDIENTS

Red chillies	15
Turmeric (*kunyit*)	2.5-cm piece
Garlic	4 cloves, peeled
Shallots	15, peeled
Candlenuts (*buah keras*)	10
Dried prawn (shrimp) paste (*belacan*)	2.5 x 5-cm piece; replaceable with 1 1/2 Tbsp dry granules
Lemon grass (*serai*)	7.5–10-cm, thinly sliced
Cooking oil	4 Tbsp
Onions	2, peeled and diced
Salt	2 tsp
Chicken	1.5 kg, cut into bite-size pieces
Coconut cream	250 ml, squeezed from 1 grated coconut and sufficient water
Coconut milk	750 ml, squeezed from the same grated coconut and sufficient water
Kalamansi lime juice	from 2 limes

METHOD

- Grind or blend (process) chillies, turmeric, garlic, shallots, candlenuts, shrimp paste and lemon grass together. Set aside.
- Heat oil in a wok. Lightly brown onions with salt. Add ground ingredients. Fry until fragrant. Splash coconut cream to prevent ingredients from sticking to wok.
- Add chicken and fry well. Add coconut milk. Simmer until chicken is tender.
- Add coconut cream. Wait for curry to boil. Add lime juice.
- Serve curry with Roti Jala (p. 154), Steamed Flower Buns (p. 140) or plain bread rolls.

CHICKEN CURRY

INGREDIENTS

Shallots	250 g, peeled and chopped
Candlenuts (*buah keras*)	5–6
Lemon grass (*serai*)	1 stalk
Dried chillies	10, soaked
Curry powder (p. 109)	5 Tbsp
Salt	1 tsp and more to taste
Cooking oil	55 ml
Coconut cream	250 ml, squeezed from 1 grated coconut and sufficient water
Coconut milk	1.25 litres, squeezed from same grated coconut and sufficient water
Chicken	1.5 kg, cut into bite-size pieces

METHOD

- Grind or blend (process) shallots, candlenuts, lemon grass and chillies together.
- Mix ground ingredients with curry powder and 1 tsp salt.
- Heat oil in a wok. Fry curry-powder mixture until fragrant. Add 2 Tbsp coconut cream to prevent drying.
- Add chicken. Fry a while. Add 2–3 Tbsp coconut milk to prevent ingredients from sticking to the wok.
- Add remaining coconut milk. Simmer until chicken is tender. Add remaining coconut cream. Adjust to taste with salt.
- Dish out. Serve with Nasi Kunyit (p. 139).

Preparation time: 30 minutes; Cooking time: 60 minutes
Serves 8

HOKKIEN NASI MINYAK

Nasi minyak translates into "oily rice" from Malay. Yet, Hokkien is a Chinese dialect and ethnic group.

INGREDIENTS

Cooking oil	6 Tbsp
Shallots	90 g, peeled and sliced
Dried prawns (shrimps) (*haebe*)	90 g, washed and soaked
Dried Chinese mushrooms	15 g, soaked, stems discarded and cut into strips
Pepper	1/2 tsp
Belly pork	300 g, parboiled and cut into thin strips
Dark soy sauce	2 tsp
Glutinous rice	1.25 kg, soaked for 60 minutes
Salt	1 tsp
Water	1.1 litres
Monosodium glutamate (optional)	1 tsp
Spring onion (scallion)	1 stalk, thinly sliced
Red chilli	1, seeded and cut into thin strips

METHOD

- Heat oil in a wok. Fry shallots until crisp. Drain and set aside.
- In the same hot oil, fry dried prawns, mushrooms and pepper until fragrant. Add pork and dark soy sauce. Fry well.
- Add glutinous rice and salt. Fry well. Add water and monosodium glutamate. Mix well.
- Cover wok. Leave to cook for 10 minutes. Then, lower heat and simmer for 25 minutes.
- Turn heat off. Add half the crispy shallots. Mix thoroughly. Transfer onto serving plate. With oiled hands, shape into firm mound.
- Garnish with spring onions, remaining shallots and chilli strips.

Preparation time: 60 minutes; Cooking time: 90 minutes
Makes: 38

KUIH PIE TEE

Kuih pie tee is a Peranakan or Straits Chinese snack.

Pie tee shells

INGREDIENTS

Plain (all-purpose) flour	90 g
Rice flour	1 Tbsp
Salt	1/4 tsp
Egg	1, beaten
Water	170 ml
Cooking oil for deep-frying	

METHOD

- Sift flours into a small bowl. Add salt. Stir in egg. Mix with water to make smooth, runny batter. Strain batter if lumpy.
- Heat oil in a deep pan. Warm mould in hot oil for 1 minute.
- Dip hot mould in batter, then in hot oil. Fry until shell is golden. Loosen shell from mould. Drain on absorbent paper.
- When cool, store in airtight tins until required.

Filling

INGREDIENTS:

Cooking oil	3 Tbsp
Garlic	4 cloves, peeled and minced
Turnip	450 g, peeled, finely shredded and squeezed of some excess water
Chicken or pork	240 g, diced
Peeled prawns (shrimps)	240 g, diced
Salt	1 tsp
Pepper	1/4 tsp
Monosodium glutamate (optional)	1/2 tsp
Five-spice powder	1/4 tsp
Crabmeat	90 g
Chinese lettuce	1 bunch
Crisp-fried shallot slices	
Coriander (cilantro) leaves	

METHOD:

- Heat oil in a wok. Lightly brown garlic. Add turnip and stir-fry. Add chicken or pork, prawns and seasoning (salt, pepper, monosodium glutamate and five-spice powder). Stir in crabmeat.
- Simmer until quite dry. Dish out. Leave to cool.
- Just before serving, line *pie tee* shell with small pieces of lettuce. Put in 2 tsp filling. Garnish with shallot slices and coriander leaves. Serve with chilli sauce.

Note: To make *pie tee* shells, a special mould is necessary.

noodles

MEE SIAM

INGREDIENTS

Dried chillies	30, soaked in warm water
Dried prawn (shrimp) paste (*belacan*)	2.5 x 5-cm piece
Preserved soybean paste (*tau cheo*)	3 Tbsp
Shallots	240 g
Prawns (shrimps)	900 g, small–medium, peeled and deveined
Light soy sauce	1 tsp
Salt	$^1/_2$ tsp
Pepper	1 dash
Cooking oil	3 Tbsp
Coconut milk	340 ml, squeezed from 1 grated coconut and sufficient water
Firm bean curd (*tau kwa*)	6, cut into 0.5-cm strips
Bean sprouts	300 g, washed and drained
Chinese chives (*kucai*)	150 g, cut into 5-cm lengths
Dried rice vermicelli (*beehoon*)	450 g, scalded to soften and drained
Cucumber	1, peeled and shredded
Eggs	5, made into a thin omelette then cut into strips
Red chillies	2, cut into thin strips
Kalamansi limes	10, halved

METHOD

- Grind or blend (process) dried chillies, dried prawn and soybean pastes and shallots. Set aside.
- Season prawns with light soy sauce, salt and pepper.
- Heat oil in a wok. Fry ground ingredients until fragrant with a little coconut milk. Add prawns and fry well. Add more coconut milk. Add bean curd. Keep stirring. Add remaining coconut milk. Leave to simmer.
- Add bean sprouts, Chinese chives and rice vermicelli. Mix thoroughly.
- Transfer to a serving plate. Garnish with cucumber, eggs and chillies. Serve with cut limes.

Preparation time: 60 minutes; Cooking time: 30 minutes
Serves 8

LAM MEE

INGREDIENTS

Chicken or pork	180 g, cut into strips
Prawns (shrimps)	120 g, small, peeled and deveined
Salt	1/2 tsp
Pepper	1/4 tsp
Light soy sauce	1 tsp
Corn flour (cornstarch)	1 tsp
Bean sprouts	300 g
Cooking oil	4 Tbsp
Chinese flowering cabbage (*choy sum*)	150 g
Fresh egg noodles (*mee*)	900 g
Shallots	3, peeled and sliced
Garlic	4 cloves, peeled and minced
Dried Chinese mushrooms	3, soaked, stems discarded and cut into strips
Crabmeat	60–90 g, cooked
Spring onion (scallion)	1 stalk, chopped
Red chillies	3, 1 cut into thin strips and 2 sliced

Gravy

Stock or water	900 ml
Light soy sauce	4 tsp
Dark soy sauce	1/2 tsp
Sesame oil	1 tsp
Salt	1 1/2 tsp
Pepper	1/4 tsp
Corn flour (cornstarch)	7 tsp

Sambal Belacan

Dried prawn (shrimp) paste (*belacan*)	5 x 5 x 0.5-cm piece
Red chillies	8, seeded
Kalamansi limes	3, halved and seeded

METHOD

- Combine gravy ingredients. Set aside.
- Season chicken or pork and prawns with salt, pepper, light soy sauce and corn flour. Set aside.
- Scald bean sprouts in boiling water and drain. Scald flowering cabbage in boiling water with 1 Tbsp oil added, then dish out and set aside. Scald noodles with the same water. Drain and transfer to serving plate. Mix in scalded bean sprouts.
- Heat remaining oil in a wok. Brown shallots and garlic. Add mushrooms and stir-fry a while. Add seasoned meat and prawns.
- Stir gravy mixture. Pour over ingredients in wok. Cover and bring to the boil. Mix in crabmeat. Quickly pour over noodles.
- Line sides of plate with flowering cabbage. Garnish with spring onion and chilli strips. Serve with sliced chillies and *sambal belacan.*
- To make *sambal belacan*, roast dried prawn paste in a pan until fragrant. While paste is hot, pound or blend (process) using a small hand food processor with red chillies until smooth. Then, transfer to a small dish and squeeze on lime juice.

Preparation time: 60 minutes; Cooking time: 30 minutes
Serves 8

LAM MEE

INGREDIENTS

Chicken or pork	180 g, cut into strips
Prawns (shrimps)	120 g, small, peeled and deveined
Salt	$^1/_2$ tsp
Pepper	$^1/_4$ tsp
Light soy sauce	1 tsp
Corn flour (cornstarch)	1 tsp
Bean sprouts	300 g
Cooking oil	4 Tbsp
Chinese flowering cabbage (*choy sum*)	150 g
Fresh egg noodles (*mee*)	900 g
Shallots	3, peeled and sliced
Garlic	4 cloves, peeled and minced
Dried Chinese mushrooms	3, soaked, stems discarded and cut into strips
Crabmeat	60–90 g, cooked
Spring onion (scallion)	1 stalk, chopped
Red chillies	3, 1 cut into thin strips and 2 sliced

Gravy

Stock or water	900 ml
Light soy sauce	4 tsp
Dark soy sauce	$^1/_2$ tsp
Sesame oil	1 tsp
Salt	1 $^1/_2$ tsp
Pepper	$^1/_4$ tsp
Corn flour (cornstarch)	7 tsp

Sambal Belacan

Dried prawn (shrimp) paste (*belacan*)	5 x 5 x 0.5-cm piece
Red chillies	8, seeded
Kalamansi limes	3, halved and seeded

METHOD

- Combine gravy ingredients. Set aside.
- Season chicken or pork and prawns with salt, pepper, light soy sauce and corn flour. Set aside.
- Scald bean sprouts in boiling water and drain. Scald flowering cabbage in boiling water with 1 Tbsp oil added, then dish out and set aside. Scald noodles with the same water. Drain and transfer to serving plate. Mix in scalded bean sprouts.
- Heat remaining oil in a wok. Brown shallots and garlic. Add mushrooms and stir-fry a while. Add seasoned meat and prawns.
- Stir gravy mixture. Pour over ingredients in wok. Cover and bring to the boil. Mix in crabmeat. Quickly pour over noodles.
- Line sides of plate with flowering cabbage. Garnish with spring onion and chilli strips. Serve with sliced chillies and *sambal belacan*.
- To make *sambal belacan*, roast dried prawn paste in a pan until fragrant. While paste is hot, pound or blend (process) using a small hand food processor with red chillies until smooth. Then, transfer to a small dish and squeeze on lime juice.

Preparation time: 30 minutes; Cooking time: 30 minutes
Serves 8

FRIED BEEHOON MEE

INGREDIENTS

Cooking oil	8 Tbsp
Shallots	8, peeled and sliced
Garlic	6 cloves, peeled and minced
Chinese flowering cabbage (*choy sum*)	300 g, cut into 7.5-cm lengths, stems and leaves separated
Fresh egg noodles (*mee*)	300 g
Bean sprouts	300 g
Dried rice vermicelli (*beehoon*)	300 g, soaked in water for about 15 minutes until soft and drained
Light soy sauce	1 tsp
Lean chicken or pork	300 g, cut into thin strips, then mixed with Seasoning B ingredients
Prawns (shrimps)	300 g, small–medium, peeled and deveined, then mixed with Seasoning C ingredients
Dark soy sauce	1 tsp

Seasoning A

Water	675 ml
Sugar	1/2 tsp
Dark soy sauce	2 tsp
Pepper	1 dash
Corn flour (cornstarch)	1/2 tsp

Seasoning B

Light soy sauce	1 tsp
Corn flour (cornstarch)	1 tsp
Sugar	1/2 tsp
Monosodium glutamate (optional)	1 tsp

Seasoning C

Sesame oil	1/2 tsp
Salt	1/2 tsp
Sugar	1 tsp
Pepper	1 dash

Garnishing

Red chillies	2, sliced
Spring onions (scallions)	2 stalks, finely sliced
Coriander (cilantro) leaves	1 sprig, chopped

METHOD

- Combine Seasoning A ingredients; set aside.
- Heat 5 Tbsp oil in a wok. Fry sliced shallots until light brown and crisp. Drain and set aside.
- Remove half the oil in wok. Brown one-third the minced garlic. Add flowering cabbage stems and stir-fry. Add a little water. Cover wok for 2–3 minutes. Add egg noodles. Stir-fry well. Cover wok for about 1 minute.
- Add flowering cabbage leaves. Stir-fry until cooked. Add a little more water, if necessary. Dish out.
- Reheat oil saved earlier. Brown half the remaining garlic. Add bean sprouts and stir-fry quickly. Add vermicelli. Stir briskly to prevent ingredients from sticking to the wok. Sprinkle a little water on wok's contents. Add light soy sauce. Mix well and dish out.
- Heat remaining 3 Tbsp oil in wok. Lightly brown remaining garlic. Add chicken or pork strips and stir-fry. Add prawns and fry with dark soy sauce. Cover wok until prawns are cooked.
- Stir Seasoning A mixture. Pour over wok's ingredients. Cover and bring to the boil. Dish out half the meat and prawns, leaving gravy behind.
- Add noodles to wok. Mix well. Dish out onto a large serving plate. Spread meat and prawns saved earlier over the top. Garnish and serve with *sambal belacan* (p.166)

FRIED BEEHOON WITH TROTTERS

INGREDIENTS

Lean pork	180 g, cut into thin strips
Cooking oil	3 Tbsp
Shallots	6, peeled and sliced
Garlic	5–6 cloves, peeled and minced
Salt	1/2 tsp
Cabbage leaves	8, cut into strips
Dried rice vermicelli (*beehoon*)	500g, soaked in water until soft and drained
Canned pig's trotters	1 can (390 g)
Spring onions (scallions)	3 stalks, cut into 5-cm lengths
Coriander (cilantro) leaves	2 sprigs, cut into 5-cm lengths
Red chillies	3, cut into thin strips

Seasoning

Light soy sauce	2 tsp
Sugar	1 tsp
Monosodium glutamate (optional)	1/2 tsp
Corn flour (cornstarch)	1 tsp
Pepper to taste	

Gravy

Water or stock	675 ml
Dark soy sauce	1 tsp
Sugar	1 tsp
Monosodium glutamate (optional)	1 tsp
Corn flour (cornstarch)	1 tsp

METHOD

- Season pork strips with seasoning ingredients; set aside. Combine gravy ingredients; set aside.
- Heat oil in a wok. Fry shallots until light brown and crisp. Dish out and set aside.
- Remove half the oil in wok. Add half the minced garlic to wok and fry with salt. Add cabbage and fry with a little water until cooked. Add vermicelli and mix well. Dish out to a plate.
- Reheat oil saved earlier. Brown remaining garlic. Add pork strips. Fry until fragrant. Add a little water. Cover wok until meat is cooked. Stir gravy ingredients and pour over pork. Bring to the boil.
- Add trotters. Bring to another boil. Dish out half the ingredients, leaving gravy behind.
- Add vermicelli to wok. Mix well. Dish out onto a large serving plate. Spread ingredients saved earlier over the top. Garnish with spring onions, coriander, chillies and crispy shallots.

Preparation time: 90 minutes; Cooking time: 30 minutes
Serves 8–10

PENANG LAKSA

INGREDIENTS

Dried chillies	30–40, soaked
Sliced galangal (*lengkuas*)	1 Tbsp
Dried prawn (shrimp) paste (*belacan*)	1 x 2.5 x 5-cm piece
Lemon grass (*serai*)	3 stalks, sliced
Shallots	180 g, peeled
Cooking oil	4 Tbsp
Water	1.35 litres
Sweet basil (*selasih*)	10 stalks
Torch ginger flowers (*bunga kantan*)	3–4, buds halved and stems smashed
Dried tamarind (*asam keping*)	4 pieces

METHOD

- Grind or blend (process) dried chillies, galangal, dried shrimp paste, lemon grass and shallots.
- Heat oil in a large wok. Fry ground ingredients until fragrant. Add water and bring to the boil.
- Add sweet basil, torch ginger flowers, dried tamarind and tamarind liquid. Lower heat. Simmer for 10–15 minutes.
- Add flaked fish and sugar. Add salt to taste. Remove sweet basil, torch ginger flowers and dried tamarind.
- Portion noodles into individual bowls. Add a little of each garnishing ingredient. Cover bowl's contents with boiling gravy. Drizzle 1 tsp diluted black prawn paste over the top. Serve immediately.

INGREDIENTS

Tamarind pulp (*asam Jawa*)	4 Tbsp, mixed with 225 ml water and strained
Wolf Herring (*ikan parang*)	1.8 kg, steamed and flaked
Sugar	2 Tbsp
Salt to taste	
Thick round rice (*laksa*) noodles	600 g, parboiled
Black prawn paste (*haeko*)	diluted with a little water

Garnishing

Pineapple	1/2, peeled and cut into thin strips
Cucumber	1, peeled and shredded
Lettuce	1/2 head, finely shredded
Onion	1, peeled and finely sliced
Red chillies	2–3, seeded and sliced
Mint leaves	quantity as required

anytime drinks

Preparation time: 15 minutes

ORANGE SPARKLER

INGREDIENTS

Orange squash	1.1 litres
7-Up soft drink	450 ml
Pineapple juice	1 can (540 ml)
Whisky	3 Tbsp
Orange	1, thinly sliced
Ice cubes	

METHOD

- Combine all ingredients except orange slices and ice cubes. Refrigerate.
- Just before serving, top with orange slices and add ice cubes.

TEA PUNCH

INGREDIENTS

Sugar	225 g
Water	450 ml
Strong freshly made tea	450 ml
Lemon juice	115 ml
Pineapple and orange juice	1 can (1.36 litres)
7-Up soft drink	2 bottles (1.5 litres)
Lemon	1, thinly sliced
Ice cubes	

METHOD

- Boil sugar in water until sugar dissolves. Combine all ingredients.
- Chill and garnish with lemon slices. Just before serving, add ice cubes.

FRUIT PUNCH

INGREDIENTS

Maraschino cherries	1 jar (540 g)
Orange squash	1.1 litres
Grapefruit juice	1 can (540 ml)
Pineapple juice	1 can (540 ml)
7-Up soft drink	1.5 litres
Kalamansi lime juice	from 5–6 limes
Oranges	2, thinly sliced
Ice cubes	

METHOD

- Drain cherries and reserve syrup. Set both aside.
- Except cherries, orange slices and ice cubes, combine all other ingredients, including maraschino syrup. Refrigerate.
- Just before serving, top with orange slices and cherries. Add ice cubes.